Simple
Christmas
Tidings

Kim Diehl

Simple Christmas Tidings

Scrappy Quilts and Projects for Yuletide Style

Martingale®
Create with Confidence

Simple Christmas Tidings: Scrappy Quilts
and Projects for Yuletide Style
© 2016 by Kim Diehl

Martingale®
19021 120th Ave. NE, Ste. 102
Bothell, WA 98011-9511 USA
ShopMartingale.com

Printed in China
21 20 19 18 17 16   8 7 6 5 4 3 2 1

Library of Congress Cataloging-in-Publication Data
is available upon request.

ISBN: 978-1-60468-666-1

MISSION STATEMENT

We empower makers who use fabric and yarn
to make life more enjoyable.

CREDITS

**PUBLISHER AND
CHIEF VISIONARY OFFICER**
Jennifer Erbe Keltner

CONTENT DIRECTOR
Karen Costello Soltys

DESIGN MANAGER
Adrienne Smitke

MANAGING EDITOR
Tina Cook

PRODUCTION MANAGER
Regina Girard

ACQUISITIONS EDITOR
Karen M. Burns

PHOTOGRAPHER
Brent Kane

TECHNICAL EDITOR
Laurie Baker

ILLUSTRATOR
Missy Shepler

COPY EDITOR
Sheila Chapman Ryan

SPECIAL THANKS

*Thanks to Janet Nesbitt of Reardan, Washington,
for allowing the photography for
this book to take place in her home.*

Acknowledgments

The merriest shout-out to Jennifer Martinez and Jan Ragaller for your divine piecing skills. Such incredibly perfect points and precise workmanship I've never seen, and I feel so thankful that you shared your talents with me.

A thousand yuletide blessings to my special Christmas quilting angel, Deborah Poole, for your enchanting stitches that truly made these holiday quilts and projects shine.

A holly jolly high-five to Laurie Baker for your incomparable technical knowledge, for being one of my best buds, and for the way that you effortlessly make me look smarter than I really am.

To Santa's special elves, cleverly disguised as the staff at Martingale, thank you for your expertise and guidance as we built this book together. Working with you is always like finding the best present under the tree.

To Karen Junquet and Lenny Kuperman at Henry Glass & Co., Santa most definitely has you on his "Nice" list for helping me develop the beautiful fabrics used to make the projects in this holiday book.

And last, but most certainly not least, I'd like to give a big holiday hug to Janet Nesbitt for welcoming us into your beautiful home to photograph the quilts and projects. What a perfect place to capture the magic of Christmas!

~ Kim

Contents

Introduction

Christmas comes but once a year, so what better time to pull out all the stops, share the traditions of quiltmaking, and surround the ones you love with some homemade goodness?

I've always enjoyed the crisp chill of winter and the holiday magic that comes with it—twinkling lights and evergreens, spicy scents and yummy treats, and friends and neighbors wreathed in smiles and good cheer. Best of all, it's an ideal time to show our generosity of spirit by taking up needle and thread and wrapping our homes and families in a little hand-stitched charm.

Designing and making quilts has always been near and dear to my heart, and I especially love scattering them throughout the house during the holidays. To me, quilts and Christmas are a bit like turkey and dressing, pumpkin and pie, snowflakes and mittens . . . they go hand in hand!

This collection of Christmas quilts and projects is designed to capture the spirit of the holidays, but many can be used into the months beyond. They're richly hued and comforting, perfect for brightening wintry days, and they honor our quilting heritage with time-honored blocks and motifs embraced for generations.

Because I've always been a person who feels that more is definitely more, I couldn't resist sharing a handful of recipes for my family's favorite holiday goodies and treats—and because Christmas most certainly isn't the time for restraint, my advice is to embrace the temptation, pull on your stretchy pants, and whip up some of these decadent little morsels. And to continue the idea that restraint is highly overrated, I've sprinkled in scads of little Pin Point sewing tips and Yuletide Style tips with ideas for gifting, tree trimming, decorating, and homemade crafts—plenty of ideas for making new memories and traditions with your own family.

Whether you've been naughty or nice, I wish you all the joy that Christmas brings and many blessings throughout the holidays and beyond!

~ *Kim*

Twinkle Trees Table Topper

What happens when you take sparkling scrappy stars, add cleverly placed bits of green, and stitch it all together? A tree is born! Layer this little patchwork quilt onto a tabletop or smooth it over the back of a sofa for an instant touch of merry and bright.

Materials

Yardage is based on 42" of useable fabric width after prewashing and removing selvages.

1⅜ yards of cream print for blocks

20 chubby sixteenths (9" x 11") of assorted prints for Christmas Tree blocks and center unit

½ yard of red print #1 for Red Star block centers and binding

1 fat quarter (18" x 22") of red print #2 for Red Star block points

1 fat quarter of medium-green print for Christmas Tree blocks

1 chubby sixteenth of brown print for Christmas Tree blocks

2½ yards of fabric for backing

45" x 45" square of batting

Fine-tip water-soluble marker

Cutting

Cut all pieces across the width of the fabric in the order given unless otherwise noted.

From *each* of the 20 assorted-print chubby sixteenths, cut:

17 squares, 1½" x 1½" (combined total of 340)

From the cream print, cut:

11 strips, 1½" x 42"; crosscut into:
+ 92 rectangles, 1½" x 2½"
+ 84 squares, 1½" x 1½"
+ 8 rectangles, 1½" x 5½"

5 strips, 2½" x 42"; crosscut into:
+ 8 rectangles, 2½" x 4½"
+ 12 rectangles, 2½" x 8½"
+ 20 squares, 2½" x 2½"

1 strip, 3¼" x 42"; crosscut into 10 squares, 3¼" x 3¼". Cut each square in half diagonally *once* to yield 2 triangles (combined total of 20).

2 strips, 5½" x 42"; crosscut into 8 rectangles, 5½" x 8½"

From the medium-green print, cut:

40 rectangles, 1½" x 2½"

32 squares, 1½" x 1½"

From the brown print, cut:

8 rectangles, 1½" x 2½"

From red print #1, cut:

1 strip, 4½" x 42"; crosscut into 5 squares, 4½" x 4½"

4 binding strips, 2½" x 42"

From red print #2, cut:

40 squares, 1½" x 1½"

10 squares, 3¼" x 3¼"; cut each square in half diagonally *once* to yield 2 triangles (combined total of 20)

FINISHED QUILT SIZE: 38½" x 38½"

Designed by Kim Diehl. Pieced by Jan Ragaller.
Machine quilted by Deborah Poole.

Piecing the Christmas Tree Blocks

Sew all pieces with right sides together using a ¼" seam allowance unless otherwise noted.

Making the Star-Point Units

1. Use a pencil and an acrylic ruler to draw a diagonal sewing line from corner to corner on the wrong side of 224 assorted-print 1½" squares. Reserve the remaining assorted-print 1½" squares.

2. Layer a prepared 1½" square from step 1 onto one end of a cream 1½" x 2½" rectangle. Stitch the pair together on the drawn line. Refer to "Pressing Triangle Units" on page 107 to fold, press, and trim the layers to form a star point. In the same manner layer, stitch, fold, press, and trim a second 1½" square from step 1 to the remaining end of the cream rectangle to make a mirror-image point. Repeat for a total of 52 cream flying-geese star-point units measuring 1½" x 2½", including the seam allowances. Reserve the remaining cream 1½" x 2½" rectangles.

Make 52.

3. Using the green 1½" x 2½" rectangles, repeat step 2 to make 40 green flying-geese star-point units.

Make 40.

4. Using the brown 1½" x 2½" rectangles, repeat step 2 to make four brown flying-geese star-point units. Reserve the remaining brown rectangles and prepared assorted-print 1½" squares.

Make 4.

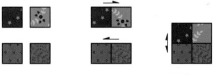

Making the Four-Patch Units

Using the reserved assorted-print 1½" squares, lay out four squares in two horizontal rows of two squares each. Join the squares in each row. Press the seam allowances in opposite directions. Join the rows. Press the seam allowances open. Repeat for a total of 28 four-patch units measuring 2½" square, including the seam allowances. Please note that you'll have four unused assorted 1½" squares; these have been included for added versatility as you piece the patchwork units.

Make 28.

Making Units A–D

1. Lay out three cream star-point units, one green star-point unit, one four-patch unit, and four cream 1½" squares in three horizontal rows as shown. Join the pieces in each row. Press the seam allowances of the top and bottom rows toward the squares. Press the seam allowances of the middle row toward the four-patch unit. Join the rows. Press the seam allowances toward the top and bottom rows. Repeat for a total of four A units measuring 4½" square, including the seam allowances.

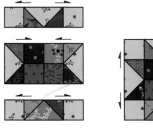

Unit A.
Make 4.

2. Lay out two cream star-point units, two green star-point units, one four-patch unit, two cream 1½" squares, and two green 1½" squares in three horizontal rows as shown. Join and press as instructed in step 1. Repeat for a total of four B units and four mirror-image B units measuring 4½" square, including the seam allowances.

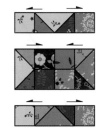

Unit B.   Unit B
                mirror image.
        Make 4 of each.

3. Lay out three cream star-point units, one green star-point unit, one four-patch unit, three cream 1½" squares, and one green 1½" square in three horizontal rows as shown. Join and press as instructed in step 1. Repeat for a total of four C units and four mirror-image C units measuring 4½" square, including the seam allowances.

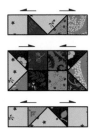

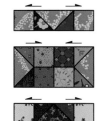

Unit C.   Unit C
                   mirror image.
        Make 4 of each.

4. Lay out three green star-point units, one brown star-point unit, one four-patch unit, two cream 1½" squares, and two green 1½" squares in three horizontal rows as shown. Join and press as instructed in step 1. Repeat for a total of four D units measuring 4½" square, including the seam allowances. Reserve the remaining four-patch units.

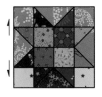

Unit D.
Make 4.

Assembling the Blocks

1. Join a cream 2½" x 4½" rectangle to each side of an A unit as shown. Press the seam allowances toward the rectangles. Repeat for a total of four single-star units measuring 4½" x 8½", including the seam allowances.

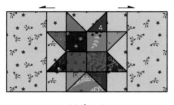

Make 4.

2. Join a B unit and a mirror-image B unit as shown. Press the seam allowances open. Repeat for a total of four double-star units measuring 4½" x 8½", including the seam allowances.

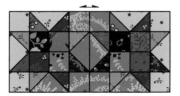

Make 4.

3. Lay out one C unit, a mirror-image C unit, and a D unit as shown. Join the blocks. Press the seam allowances open. Repeat for a total of four triple-star units measuring 4½" x 12½", including the seam allowances.

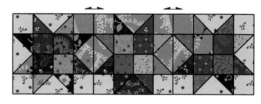

Make 4.

4. Join a cream 1½" x 5½" rectangle to each end of a reserved brown 1½" x 2½" rectangle. Press the seam allowances toward the brown. Repeat for a total of four tree-trunk units measuring 1½" x 12½", including the seam allowances.

Make 4.

5. Select two prepared assorted-print 1½" squares and a cream 2½" x 8½" rectangle. Layer, stitch, fold, press, and trim as previously instructed to form a star-point unit and a mirror-image star point on one end of the rectangle. Repeat for a total of eight rectangles measuring 2½" x 8½", including the seam allowances. Reserve the remaining cream 2½" x 8½" rectangles and the prepared assorted 1½" squares.

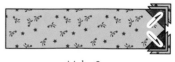

Make 8.

6. Join a single-star unit to the top of a double-star unit. Press the seam allowances toward the single-star unit. Join a rectangle from step 5 to opposite sides of the star unit as shown. Press the seam allowances toward the pieced rectangles. Repeat for a total of four tree-top units measuring 8½" x 12½", including the seam allowances.

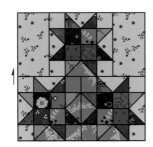

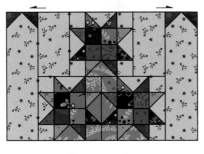

Tree-top unit.
Make 4.

7. Join a tree-trunk unit from step 4 to the bottom edge of a triple-star unit. Press the seam allowances toward the tree-trunk unit. Repeat for a total of four tree-base units measuring 5½" x 12½", including the seam allowances.

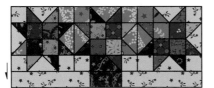

Tree-base unit.
Make 4.

8. Join the bottom edge of a tree-top unit to the top edge of a tree-base unit. Press the seam allowances toward the tree-top unit. Repeat for a total of four Christmas Tree blocks measuring 12½" x 13½", including the seam allowances.

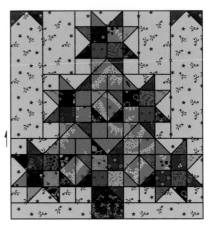

Christmas Tree block.
Make 4.

Piecing the Red Star Blocks

1. Use a pencil and an acrylic ruler to draw a diagonal sewing line from corner to corner on the wrong side of the remaining 20 cream 1½" squares and each 1½" red print #2 square.

2. Layer, stitch, fold, press, and trim a prepared cream square onto each corner of a 4½" red print #1 square as previously instructed. Repeat for a total of five snowball units measuring 4½" square, including the seam allowances.

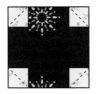

Make 5.

YULETIDE STYLE

Sugared Pecans

One of my hands-down favorite holiday treats is sugared pecans, and I'm happy to share my easy recipe for these yummy morsels. Warning: These are highly habit-forming, but if you're able to part with some of them, they make great gifts when wrapped in cellophane bags and tied up with pretty little bows.

~ Kim

2 egg whites
1 tablespoon water
1 pound pecan halves
1 cup granulated white sugar
1 teaspoon salt
¾ teaspoon ground cinnamon

Preheat oven to 250°F. Lightly grease or coat a baking sheet with nonstick cooking spray. In a gallon-sized plastic zipper bag, mix sugar, salt, and cinnamon. In a large bowl with the mixer set on high, whip egg whites and water until frothy. (This only takes about a minute!) Add pecans to whipped egg whites and stir until coated. Pour pecans into the bag of sugar mixture and toss until coated. Spread coated pecans on the prepared baking sheet and bake at 250° for one hour, stirring every 15 minutes. Serve in a bowl, or ladle cooled pecans into cellophane gift bags and tie with ribbons.

3. Stitch the cream and red print #2 triangles together along the long diagonal edges, taking care not to stretch the fabric. Press the seam allowances toward the red print. Trim away the dog-ear points. Repeat for a total of 20 half-square-triangle units.

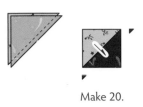

Make 20.

4. Using a rotary cutter and an acrylic ruler, cut each half-square-triangle unit in half diagonally through the sewn center seam to make a total of 40 pieced triangles.

Make 40 total.

5. Join two pieced triangles as shown to make an hourglass unit. Press the seam allowances open. Trim away the dog-ear points. Repeat for a total of 20 hourglass units measuring 2½" square, including the seam allowances.

Make 20.

6. Layer, stitch, fold, press, and trim a prepared 1½" red print #2 square onto one end of a reserved cream 1½" x 2½" rectangle as previously instructed. Repeat for a total of 20 pieced rectangles and 20 pieced mirror-image rectangles measuring 1½" x 2½", including the seam allowances.

Make 20 of each.

7. Join a pieced rectangle and a pieced mirror-image rectangle to the red sides of an hourglass unit as shown. Press the seam allowances toward the rectangles. Repeat for a total of 20 side units measuring 2½" x 4½", including the seam allowances.

Make 20.

8. Lay out one snowball unit, four side units, and four cream 2½" squares in three horizontal rows as shown. Join the pieces in each row. Press the seam allowances toward the cream squares and snowball unit. Join the rows. Press the seam allowances away from the middle row. Repeat for a total of five Red

Star blocks measuring 8½" square, including the seam allowances.

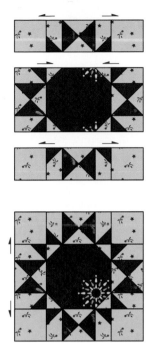

Make 5.

Piecing the Quilt Top

1. Join a cream 5½" x 8½" rectangle to two adjacent sides of a Red Star block as shown. Press the seam allowances toward the rectangles. Repeat for a total of four Red Star corner blocks measuring 13½" x 13½", including the seam allowances. Don't be concerned about the open corner areas of the blocks; they'll be trimmed away after the top has been pieced and quilted.

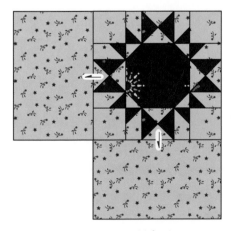

Make 4.

2. Using a reserved cream 2½" x 8½" rectangle and four reserved prepared assorted 1½" squares, layer, stitch, fold, press, and trim to add two star points on each end of the rectangle to make a sashing rectangle. Repeat for a total of four sashing rectangles measuring 2½" x 8½", including the seam allowances.

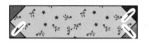

Make 4.

3. Lay out four reserved four-patch units, four sashing rectangles, and the remaining Red Star block in three horizontal rows as shown. Join the pieces in each row. Press the seam allowances toward the sashing rectangles. Join the rows. Press the seam allowances away from the middle row. The pieced center unit should measure 12½" square, including the seam allowances.

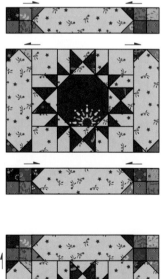
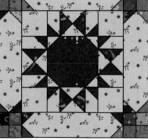

Make 1.

4. Lay out the four Red Star corner blocks, the four tree units, and the center unit in three horizontal rows as shown below. Join the pieces in each row. Press the seam allowances away from the tree units. Join the rows. Press the seam allowances toward the middle row.

PIN POINT

Tree Skirt Option

While this pattern works beautifully as a table topper, it would make an equally excellent tree skirt. To adapt this project, simply substitute an 8½" square of your background print for the center Red Star block when piecing the top. Follow the guidelines provided on page 74 of the "Holiday Hospitality Tree Skirt" project to add the center and side openings and attach the tie, and you've got yourself a tree skirt!

Quilt assembly

Completing the Quilt

1. Using a water-soluble marker and a long acrylic ruler (or you can place two shorter rulers together end to end to achieve the needed length) and referring to the pictured quilt, draw a diagonal line from corner to corner of the tree units, ensuring that the drawn lines fall approximately ¼" beyond the pieced points of each Red Star corner block.

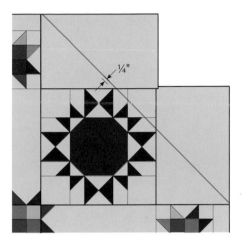

2. Layer the quilt top, batting, and backing. Quilt the layers, keeping the quilting on each corner within the drawn diagonal lines. The featured quilt was machine quilted with repeating diagonal lines radiating out from the center of the green Christmas tree areas, and intersecting diagonal lines were stitched from point to point on the stars. The Red Star blocks were stitched with arced lines on the red and cream triangles, and a small diagonal crosshatch was quilted onto each red center square. A curling vine and teardrop leaf pattern was used to fill the background areas.

3. Trim away the excess batting and backing, cutting along the drawn lines at each corner.

4. Join the four red print #1 strips into one length and use it to bind the quilt.

Snowman Shenanigans Wall Hanging

Who knows what mischief snowmen are up to while we're snug in our beds and fast sleep—playing hide 'n' seek or ding-dong ditch, maybe even swinging from the trees and catching snowflakes! The magic of Christmas makes anything possible.

Materials

Yardage is based on 42" of useable fabric width after prewashing and removing selvages.

1 yard of dark-blue print for sky and binding

8 chubby sixteenths (9" x 11") of assorted prints for patchwork border

⅓ yard of tan print for patchwork border

5 rectangles, 6" x 10", of assorted beige wools for snowmen appliqués (use a slightly larger piece if you choose to cut your snowmen from the bias to take advantage of plaid and check patterns)

¼ yard (not a fat quarter) of medium-green print for upper grass appliqué

¼ yard (not a fat quarter) of dark-green print for lower grass appliqué

2 fat eighths (9" x 22") of similar brown prints for tree appliqués

1 chubby sixteenth *each* of orange, gold, black, and blue prints for chimney, roof, window, and door appliqués (respectively) and patchwork border

1 fat eighth of red stripe or print for house appliqué and patchwork border

1 chubby sixteenth of light-tan print for pathway appliqué

1" x 12" rectangle *each* of 5 assorted wools for scarves

1 charm square (5" x 5") of orange wool for nose appliqués

Supplies for your favorite traditional- and wool-appliqué method. If you're using my wool-appliqué method, you'll need approximately ½ yard of 17"-wide lightweight, paper-backed fusible web (I like HeatnBond Lite).

#8 or #12 perle cotton in beige, brown, and black for stitching wool appliqués (I used Valdani's #12 perle cotton in variegated P3 Aged White to appliqué the snowmen, solid black for French knot eyes, and assorted variegated shades of brown for twig arms.)

Orange all-purpose thread to match carrot noses

Small buttons: 26 assorted white buttons for snowflakes; 17 assorted tan, brown, and black buttons for snowmen fronts; and 2 buttons for doorknob and doorbell

Size 5 embroidery needle

Freezer paper

1¼ yards of fabric for backing

34" x 43" piece of batting

Cutting

Cut all pieces across the width of the fabric in the order given unless otherwise noted. For greater ease, cutting instructions for the appliqués are provided separately.

From the dark-blue print, cut:
1 rectangle, 21½" x 26½"
4 binding strips, 2½" x 42"

From the dark-green print, cut:
1 rectangle, 4½" x 21½"

From the tan print, cut:
156 squares, 1½" x 1½"

From *each* of the orange, gold, black, and blue chubby sixteenths; and *each* of the 8 assorted print chubby sixteenths; and the red stripe, cut:
3 squares, 3½" x 3½" (combined total of 39). Reserve the remainder of the orange, gold, black, and blue prints for the house appliqués.

FINISHED QUILT SIZE: 27½" x 36½"

Designed, pieced, and machine and hand appliquéd by Kim Diehl.
Machine quilted by Deborah Poole.

Piecing the Quilt Center and Adding the Cotton Appliqués

Sew all pieces with right sides together using a ¼" seam allowance unless otherwise noted. Refer to "Invisible Machine Appliqué" on page 107 for complete step-by-step appliqué instructions, or use your own favorite method. Prepare the appliqués from the cotton fabrics indicated in "Materials" on page 22. Appliqué patterns are on pages 31–37. Note that for this project it isn't necessary to add and turn under seam allowances along any appliqué edge that rests along the outer perimeter of the quilt top; the seam allowance has been included in these pieces, and the raw edges will be enclosed within the seams when the border is added.

1. Join the dark-green 4½" x 21½" rectangle to the dark-blue 21½" x 26½" rectangle along the 21½" edges. Press the seam allowances toward the dark green.

2. Trace the upper grass patterns on pages 31 and 32 onto freezer paper. Cut out the pieces and tape them together to form the upper grass section. Prepare and stitch the appliqué, positioning the bottom edge approximately 3¼" up from the bottom edge of the background, and remembering that there's no need to add and turn under seam allowances on the right and left sides of the grass piece. Remember to leave the top portion of the grass unstitched where indicated to enable the snowman to be added when the wool appliqués are stitched.

3. Referring to the quilt pictured on page 24, prepare and stitch the pathway appliqué, aligning the left and bottom raw edges with the lower-left corner edges of the background to perfectly position it.

4. Using a rotary cutter and acrylic ruler, cut the following house components from freezer paper:
   • 1 rectangle, 4¼" x 18" (house)
   • 1 rectangle, 2¼" x 10½" (door)
   • 1 rectangle, 4" x 5¼" (roof)
   • 1 rectangle, 1" x 4½" (chimney)
   • 2 rectangles, 1" x 3" (windows)

5. To add the angle to the right edge of the roof, fold over the right edge of the 4" x 5¼" freezer-paper rectangle 2" and finger-press a crease. Use a rotary cutter and an acrylic ruler to cut away the upper corner from the upper-edge crease to the bottom-right corner.

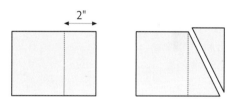

6. Prepare the house appliqués from the designated fabrics, remembering that the left edges of the house, roof, and door don't need to be turned under because these raw edges will be enclosed within the seam when the border is added.

7. Referring to the pictured quilt, align the left edge of the house with the left edge of the background, placing the bottom edge of the house approximately 5¼" up from the bottom of the background and ensuring the top of the pathway is overlapped at least ¼". Appliqué the house in place and carefully remove the freezer-paper pattern, leaving an approximate 7" opening on the right side of the house, beginning about ½" up, to enable the snowman to be added later.

8. Using the pictured quilt as a guide, continue working from the bottom layer to the top to add the chimney, roof, windows, and door, remembering to remove the freezer-paper patterns after each layer is added.

9. Trace, cut, and use tape to assemble the tree branch and trunk pattern pieces on pages 34, 36, and 37 from freezer paper. Referring to the photo, prepare the branch and trunk appliqués from the designated prints, making one and one reversed appliqué piece of branch #2 and one of each of the remaining pieces.

10. Using the pictured quilt as a guide, lay out the branch #1 piece, aligning the short ends with the background top and right-hand raw edges to perfectly position it; pin in place. Position the branch #2 and #2 reversed pieces on the background in a way that pleases you, tucking the raw ends underneath piece #1 approximately ¼". Remove piece #1 and appliqué pieces #2 and #3 in place; remove the freezer-paper patterns. Reposition, baste, and stitch tree piece #1; remove the freezer-paper pattern.

11. Position, baste, and stitch branch pieces #3 and #4 and trunk piece #1 in numeric order, aligning the right raw edge with the background right edge. Remove the freezer-paper pattern pieces after adding each layer. Reserve tree trunk #2, as it will be stitched after the snowman has been added.

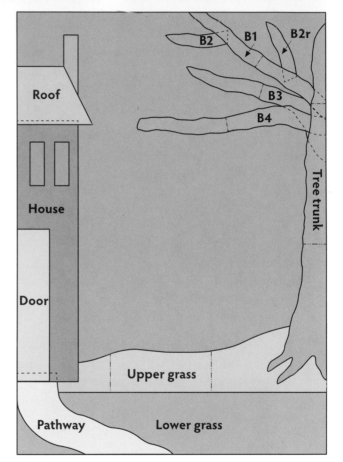

Placement diagram

Preparing and Adding the Wool Appliqués

Please refer to "Wool Appliqué" on page 115 for complete step-by-step appliqué instructions, or use your own favorite method. Remember that for non-symmetrical shapes, the wool-appliqué method featured in this project will produce a finished appliqué that is reversed from the shape provided on the pattern sheet. Patterns for the wool appliqués are on page 35.

1. Using the assorted beige wools for the snowmen and the orange wool for the carrot noses, prepare the appliqués indicated below, modifying the patterns as shown on the pattern sheet.
   - 1 *each* of snowman A and A reversed
   - 1 *each* of snowman B and B reversed
   - 1 of snowman C
   - 5 carrot noses

2. To prepare the scarves, use an awl or a sturdy straight pin to catch and remove a couple of threads along each long side of the assorted wool 1" x 12" rectangles. To form the fringe, use the same technique to remove several threads at each end until you're pleased with the look.

3. Using the pictured quilt as a guide, position the snowmen on the background, tucking a scarf under the neck of each one and inserting the appropriate edges of the snowmen into the openings along the house and upper grass section approximately ¼". Use the reserved trunk #2 piece to help position a snowman so he'll be peeking out from the tree on the right-hand side of the quilt. Baste the snowmen in place. Appliqué the openings where the snowmen have been inserted. Remove the trunk #2 piece. Appliqué each of the snowmen in place, stitching through the scarves along the necks to secure them. Position trunk #2 back on the background and appliqué it in place.

4. Stitch a carrot nose to each snowman. Referring to "Decorative Stitches" on page 118, use the black perle cotton to add French knot eyes. The pieced and appliquéd quilt center should measure 21½" x 30½", including the seam allowances.

Piecing and Adding the Border

1. Using a pencil and an acrylic ruler, draw a diagonal sewing line from corner to corner on the wrong side of each tan 1½" square.

2. Layer a prepared tan 1½" square onto one corner of a print 3½" square. Stitch the pair together on the drawn line. Refer to "Pressing Triangle Units" on page 107 to fold, press, and trim the layers. In the same manner layer, stitch, fold, press, and trim

to add a tan 1½" square to each remaining corner of the print square. Repeat to make a total of 39 Snowball blocks measuring 3½" square, including the seam allowances.

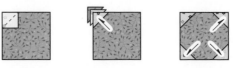

Make 39.

YULETIDE STYLE

Holiday Sparkle

Here's a super-quick and easy do-it-yourself project to add a little sparkle to your Christmas table. Rescue some of your orphaned glassware (stemless wine goblets work beautifully) or gather jars in a variety of sizes from your cupboard or a secondhand store. Spread a generous layer of Mod Podge on the outside of the jars (I use the glossy style), and then coat firmly with Epsom salt. For even more sparkle, try adding a pinch or two of glitter to the salt. After drying, add votive candles or bits of greenery and ornaments and mingle these among your table decor. Fa la la la la . . . .

3. Lay out 10 Snowball blocks end to end. Join the blocks. Press the seam allowances to one side, with each seam facing the direction that will result in the best tan point between the blocks. Repeat for a total of two pieced long border rows. Join these rows to the right and left sides of the quilt center. Press the seam allowances toward the quilt center.

Make 2.

4. Using two sets of nine Snowball blocks, repeat step 3 to piece and add two short border rows to the top and bottom of the quilt top. You'll have one unused Snowball block; this block has been included for added versatility. The pieced and appliquéd quilt top should now measure 27½" x 36½", including the seam allowances.

Completing the Quilt

1. Pin the scarves to the centers of the snowmen so they'll be away from the areas to be quilted. Layer the quilt top, batting, and backing. Quilt the layers. The featured quilt was machine quilted with a stipple pattern in the sky areas, straight lines were quilted onto the house (using the stripes as a guide), and an elongated X was stitched onto the door. The windows and chimney were outlined to emphasize their shapes. Round pebbles were stitched onto the pathway and free-form lines were quilted onto the tree and grass areas for texture. Intersecting diagonal lines were quilted onto each Snowball block to form an asterisk design and outlined along the seams of the dark edges.

2. After the top has been quilted, and using the pictured quilt as a guide, refer to "Decorative Stitches" on page 118 to stem stitch free-form twig arms for each snowman, burying the thread knots within the quilt layers.

3. Sew a sprinkling of white buttons to the sky to form snowflakes and stitch assorted tan, brown, and black buttons to the snowmen. Last, stitch the doorbell and doorknob buttons to the house, burying the thread knots within the quilt layers or leaving decorative thread tails as I did.

4. Join the dark-blue strips into one length and use it to bind the quilt.

YULETIDE STYLE

Chocolate Chip Snowball Cookies

Years ago when I was craving a big, soft chocolate chip cookie, I created this recipe, and then spent years tweaking the ingredients to get it just right. While these are great straight out of the oven, they become very soft and almost cake like when stored in an airtight container for a day . . . that is, if you can find the willpower to wait!

~Kim

2 cups granulated sugar

1 cup (2 sticks) butter, softened

8 ounces Neufchatel cheese or cream cheese

¼ cup sour cream (I use light)

4 eggs

2 teaspoons vanilla

½ teaspoon almond extract

7 cups flour

4 teaspoons baking powder

1 teaspoon baking soda

1 teaspoon salt

1 bag (11.5 ounces) milk chocolate chips (or even more, if you'd like to be decadent)

⅓ cup additional granulated sugar for rolling

Preheat oven to 375°F. In a large mixer bowl, beat 2 cups sugar, butter, Neufchatel cheese, and sour cream on medium speed until fluffy. Beat in eggs, one at a time, until combined. Stir in vanilla and almond extract. In a separate bowl, combine flour, baking powder, baking soda, and salt; add to wet mixture in three additions, beating well after each addition. Stir in chocolate chips. Cover dough with plastic wrap and refrigerate one hour. Roll dough into ping-pong-ball sized balls, and then roll in granulated sugar to coat; place 2" apart on ungreased cookie sheets. Bake for approximately 10 minutes, or just until set and very lightly browned on the bottom—don't overbake! Makes about 5 dozen soft and yummy cookies, depending upon the size you roll them.

Align with quilt center right edge.
Do not add seam allowance to this edge if
you're using a turned-edge appliqué method.

Upper grass
Right section

Pattern does not include
seam allowances.

Join to upper grass middle-section pattern.

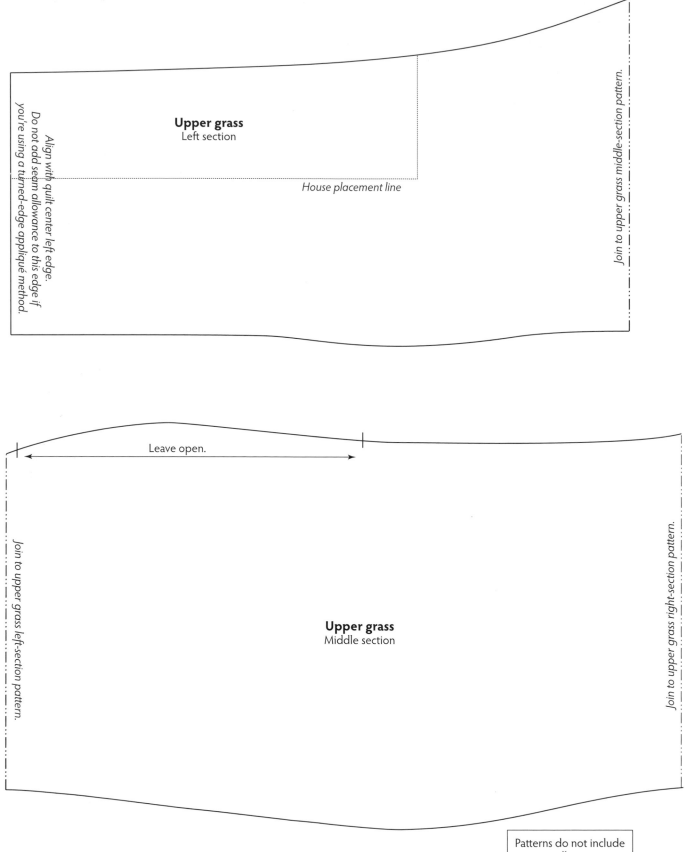

Upper grass
Left section

*Align with quilt center left edge.
Do not add seam allowance to this edge if
you're using a turned-edge appliqué method.*

House placement line

Join to upper grass middle-section pattern.

Leave open.

Upper grass
Middle section

Join to upper grass left-section pattern.

Join to upper grass right-section pattern.

Patterns do not include
seam allowances.

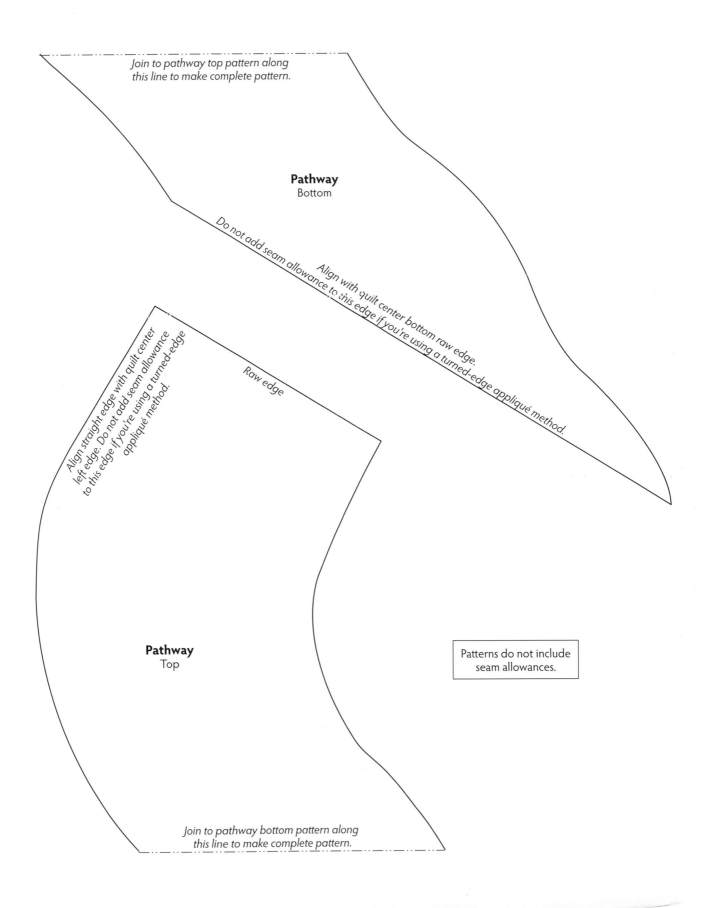

*Join to pathway top pattern along
this line to make complete pattern.*

Pathway
Bottom

Do not add seam allowance to this edge if you're using a turned-edge appliqué method.

Align with quilt center bottom raw edge.

Align straight edge with quilt center left edge. Do not add seam allowance to this edge if you're using a turned-edge appliqué method.

Raw edge

Pathway
Top

Patterns do not include
seam allowances.

*Join to pathway bottom pattern along
this line to make complete pattern.*

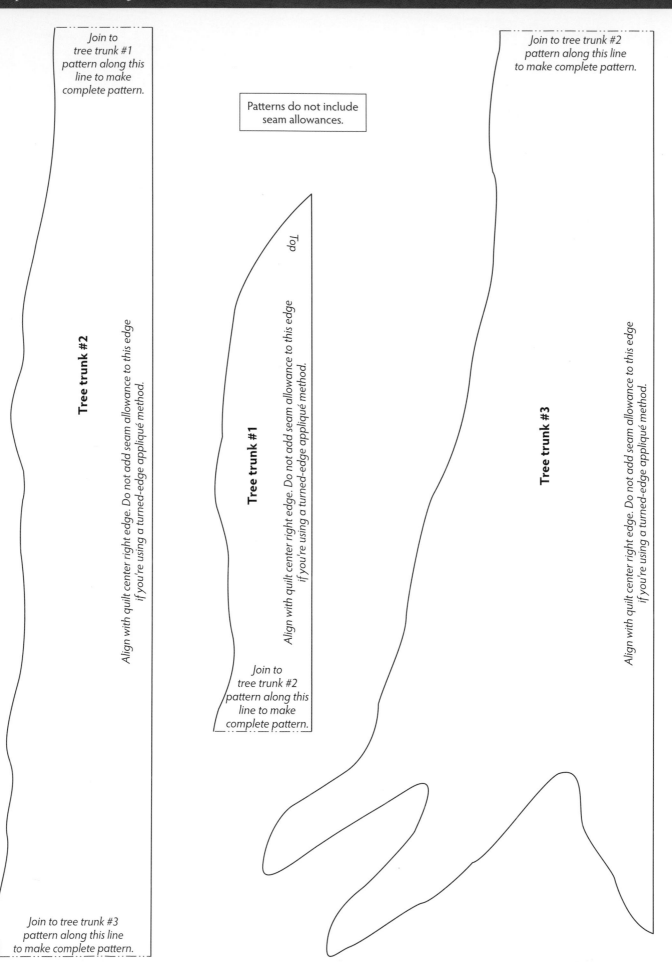

Join to tree trunk #1 pattern along this line to make complete pattern.

Patterns do not include seam allowances.

Join to tree trunk #2 pattern along this line to make complete pattern.

Tree trunk #2

Align with quilt center right edge. Do not add seam allowance to this edge if you're using a turned-edge appliqué method.

Top

Tree trunk #1

Align with quilt center right edge. Do not add seam allowance to this edge if you're using a turned-edge appliqué method.

Join to tree trunk #2 pattern along this line to make complete pattern.

Tree trunk #3

Align with quilt center right edge. Do not add seam allowance to this edge if you're using a turned-edge appliqué method.

Join to tree trunk #3 pattern along this line to make complete pattern.

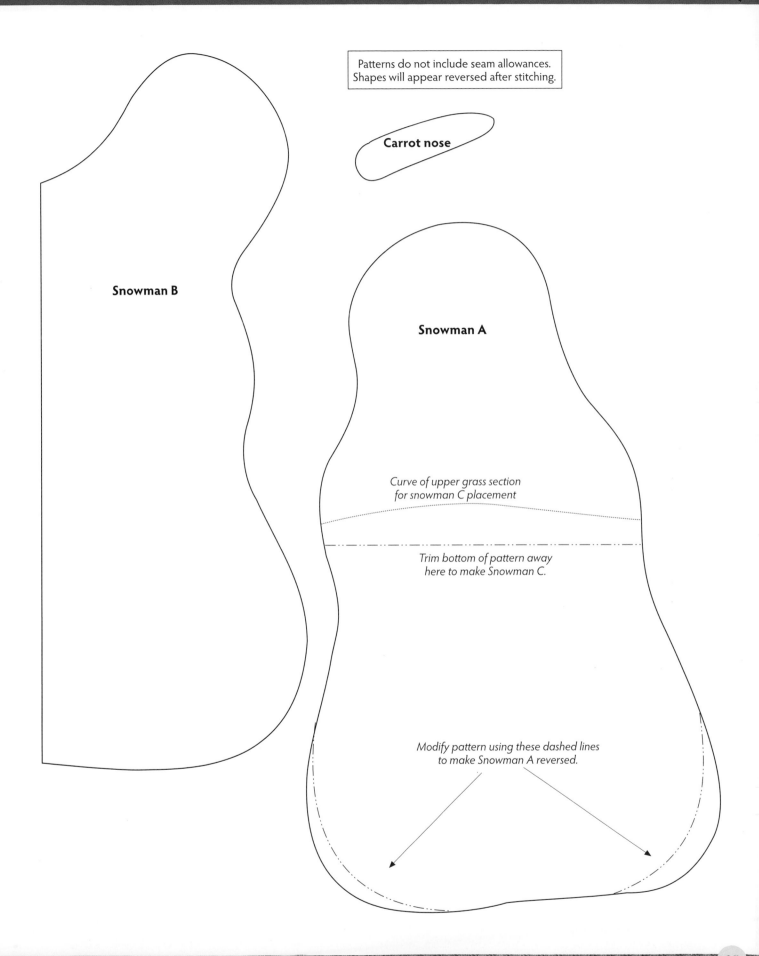

Patterns do not include seam allowances.
Shapes will appear reversed after stitching.

Carrot nose

Snowman B

Snowman A

*Curve of upper grass section
for snowman C placement*

*Trim bottom of pattern away
here to make Snowman C.*

*Modify pattern using these dashed lines
to make Snowman A reversed.*

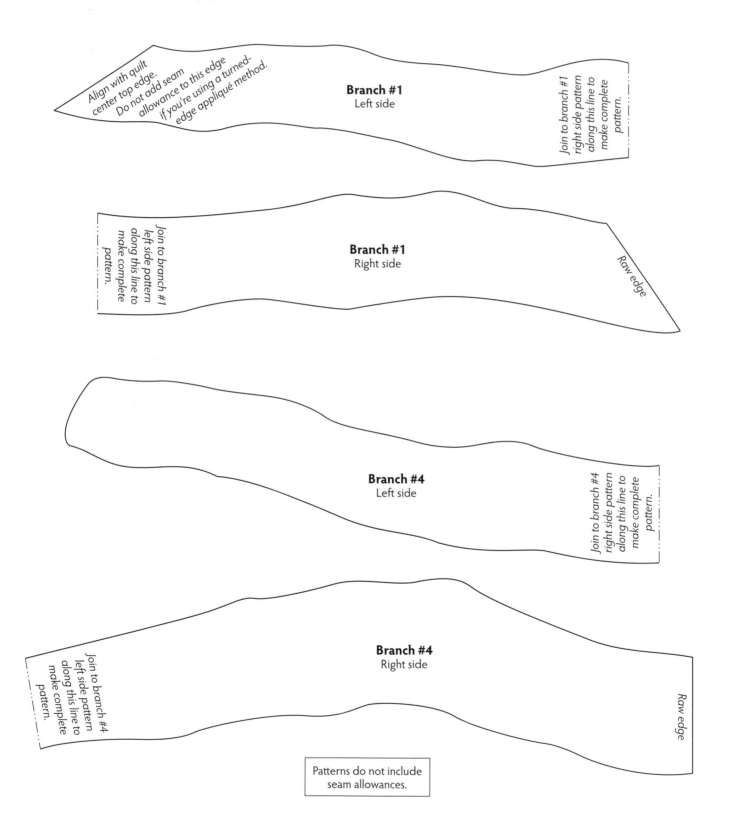

Align with quilt center top edge. Do not add seam allowance to this edge if you're using a turned-edge appliqué method.

Branch #1
Left side

Join to branch #1 right side pattern along this line to make complete pattern.

Branch #1
Right side

Join to branch #1 left side pattern along this line to make complete pattern.

Raw edge

Branch #4
Left side

Join to branch #4 right side pattern along this line to make complete pattern.

Branch #4
Right side

Join to branch #4 left side pattern along this line to make complete pattern.

Raw edge

Patterns do not include
seam allowances.

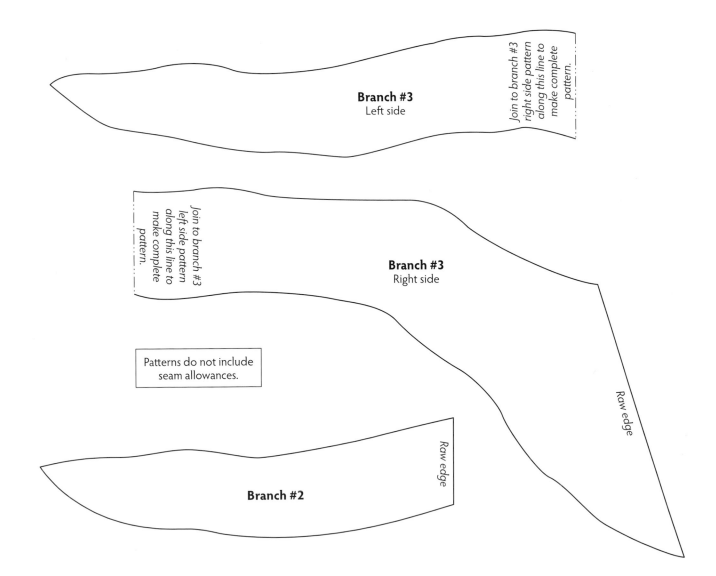

Branch #3
Left side

Join to branch #3 right side pattern along this line to make complete pattern.

Join to branch #3 left side pattern along this line to make complete pattern.

Branch #3
Right side

Patterns do not include seam allowances.

Raw edge

Raw edge

Branch #2

Twilight Star Medallion Lap Quilt

A big and sparkly patchwork star, fashioned from Christmas colors of red, green, and cheddar, is just the thing for snuggling under as you write your letter to Santa. Add a plate of cookies (some for Santa and some for you) and a big glass of milk, and you're sure to be on the nice list.

Materials

Yardage is based on 42" of useable fabric width after prewashing and removing selvages.

2⅝ yards of tan print for patchwork
1⅔ yards of red print for patchwork
1¼ yards of green print for patchwork and binding
1 yard of cheddar or gold print for patchwork
3¾ yards of fabric for backing
67" x 67" square of batting

Cutting

Cut all pieces across the width of the fabric in the order given unless otherwise noted.

From the tan print, cut:
6 strips, 10½" x 42"; crosscut into:
- 12 squares, 10½" x 10½"
- 4 rectangles, 10½" x 20½"
2 strips, 10⅞" x 42"; crosscut into 6 squares, 10⅞" x 10⅞". Cut each square in half diagonally *once* to yield two triangles (combined total of 12).

From the red print, cut:
5 strips, 10½" x 42"; crosscut into:
- 4 rectangles, 10½" x 20½"
- 8 squares, 10½" x 10½"
1 strip, 10⅞" x 42"; crosscut into 2 squares, 10⅞" x 10⅞". Cut each square in half diagonally *once* to yield 2 triangles (combined total of 4).

From the cheddar or gold print, cut:
1 strip, 20½" x 42"; crosscut into:
- 1 square, 20½" x 20½"
- 1 square, 10½" x 10½"
1 strip, 10½" x 42"; crosscut into 3 squares, 10½" x 10½"

From the green print, cut:
2 strips, 10⅞" x 42"; crosscut into 4 squares, 10⅞" x 10⅞". Cut each square in half diagonally *once* to yield 2 triangles (combined total of 8).
7 binding strips, 2½" x 42"

Piecing the Quilt Top

Sew all pieces with right sides together using a ¼" seam allowance unless otherwise noted.

1. Using a pencil and an acrylic ruler, draw a diagonal sewing line from corner to corner on the wrong side of each tan and red 10½" square. Reserve the red squares for later use.

2. Layer a prepared tan square onto one corner of the cheddar 20½" square. Stitch the pair together on the drawn line. Refer to "Pressing Triangle Units" on page 107 to fold, press, and trim the layers. In the same manner, stitch a prepared tan square to the remaining corners of the cheddar square to make a square-in-a-square unit.

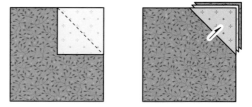

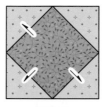

Make 1.

FINISHED QUILT SIZE: 60½" x 60½"

Designed by Kim Diehl. Pieced by Jennifer Martinez.
Machine quilted by Deborah Poole.

YULETIDE STYLE

Fresh Fruit for Tree Trimming

I love drawing from nature to decorate my tree for the holidays, because it lends an air of old-fashioned charm—and it's easy to do! Try slicing apples (approximately ⅛" thick) and thick-skinned fresh oranges (approximately ¼" thick), and then using a food dehydrator to completely dry the fruit. Poke a short length of green florist wire through the fruit near one edge and twist the ends together once or twice to hang on the tree branches. These can be reused for several years if stored in an airtight container lined with waxed paper (I recycle my used Christmas tins for this purpose).

Another time-honored tradition is freshly strung cranberries, and this is great fun to do as a family. I hand out size 5 embroidery needles threaded with long lengths of perle cotton (quadruple knotted at the ends) and bowls of fresh cranberries. Add Christmas carols, mulled cider, and yummy treats, and this is a recipe for making memories. Finished cranberry strings can be hung on the tree, swagged from chandeliers, or mingled into wreaths and garlands for a little home-fashioned charm.

3. Layer a prepared tan 10½" square onto one end of a red 10½" x 20½" rectangle. Stitch, fold, press, and trim as instructed in step 2 to form a star point. In the same manner, stitch a second tan 10½" square to the remaining end of the red rectangle to form a mirror-image point. Repeat for a total of four red flying-geese star-point units.

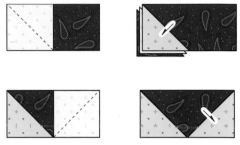

Make 4.

4. Using the reserved prepared red 10½" squares and the tan 10½" x 20½" rectangles, repeat step 3 to make four tan flying-geese star-point units.

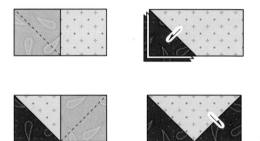

Make 4.

5. Join a tan and red 10⅞" triangle along the long diagonal edges. Press the seam allowances toward the red print. Trim away the dog-ear points. Repeat for a total of four red half-square-triangle units measuring 10½" square, including the seam allowances.

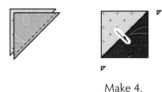

Make 4.

6. Using the tan and green 10⅞" triangles, repeat step 5 for a total of eight green half-square-triangle units measuring 10½" square, including the seam allowances.

7. Lay out two cheddar 10½" squares, two green half-square-triangle units, and one tan flying-geese

star-point unit in one horizontal row as shown. Join the units. Press the seam allowances toward each end. Repeat for a total of two A rows measuring 10½" x 60½", including the seam allowances.

Row A.
Make 2.

8. Lay out two green half-square-triangle units, two red half-square-triangle units, and one red flying-geese star-point unit in one horizontal row as shown. Join the units. Press the seam allowances toward the flying-geese star-point unit. Repeat for a total of two B rows measuring 10½" x 60½", including the seam allowances.

Row B.
Make 2.

9. Lay out two tan star-point units, two red star-point units, and the square-in-a-square unit in one horizontal row as shown. Join the units. Press the seam allowances toward each end. The C row should measure 20½" x 60½", including the seam allowances.

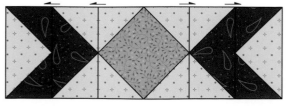

Row C.
Make 1.

10. Lay out the rows as shown to form the star medallion design. Join the rows. Press the seam allowances away from the C row. The pieced quilt top should measure 60½" square, including the seam allowances.

Completing the Quilt

Layer the quilt top, batting, and backing. Quilt the layers. The featured quilt was machine quilted with a variety of feathered motifs in the red, green, and cheddar portions of the quilt. The tan background areas were quilted with a diagonal repeating pattern of two narrow lines and one wide line, with a small-scale curling vine-and-leaf design stitched down the center of each wide line space. Join the green 2½" x 42" strips into one length and use it to bind the quilt.

Bonus Twilight Star Medallion Bed Quilt

FINISHED QUILT SIZE:
90½" x 90½"

With the addition of some simple strips and squares, this lap quilt can easily be adapted for use on a full- or queen-size bed. Refer to the chart below for the additional fabric yardage needed and the number of pieces to cut, and use the illustration as a piecing guide.

Fabric	Additional Yardage	Additional Cutting
Red print	2 yards	4 strips, 5½" x 30½"
		4 strips, 5½" x 35½"
		4 strips, 5½" x 40½"
Green print	2¼ yards	4 strips, 5½" x 30½"
		4 strips, 5½" x 35½"
		4 strips, 5½" x 40½"
		2 binding strips, 2½" x 42" (9 total)
Cheddar or gold print	⅜ yard	12 squares, 5½" x 5½"

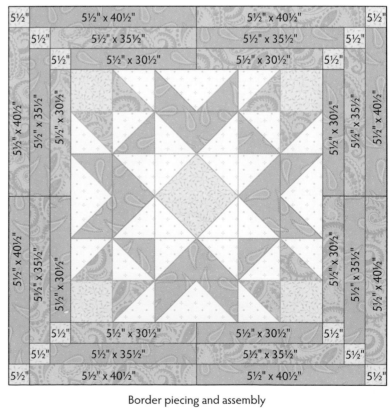

Border piecing and assembly

Welcome Home Holiday Hangers

Quilted hangers are an ideal way to add an unexpected touch of color and charm to a place that can sometimes be a challenge to decorate—your front door! Perfect for gift giving, these little hangers feature ribbon ties to make them even more versatile, bringing endless possibilities for using them all through your home.

FINISHED HANGER SIZE:

4" x 13" (excluding ribbon)

Designed, pieced, hand appliquéd, and hand quilted in the big-stitch method by Kim Diehl.

Materials

Refer to "Cutting Bias Strips" on page 105 to cut bias strips.

For each hanger

1 fat quarter (18" x 22") of cream print for hanger front and back

5" x 14" rectangle of batting

⅔ yard of 1½"-wide wired ribbon in a color to complement your hanger

Fine-tip water-soluble marker

Supplies for your favorite traditional- and wool-appliqué methods

Liquid glue for fabric, water soluble and acid free

#8 or #12 perle cotton for stitching wool appliqués and big-stitch hand quilting (Kim used Valdani's #12 perle cotton in H212 Faded Brown)

Size 5 embroidery needle

Fiberfill

For "Hospitality" hanger

1 chubby sixteenth (9" x 11") of red print for star

1" x 3" rectangle of green print for stem

5" x 5" rectangle of gold wool for pineapple appliqué

Scraps of assorted wools, including green, for leaf and penny appliqués

For "Holly" hanger

1" x 12" *bias* strip of green print for stem

Scraps of assorted green, gold, and cranberry wools for leaf, star, and berry appliqués

Assorted red buttons in a variety of sizes for berries

Bias bar to make ¼"-wide stem

Hospitality Door Hanger

Cutting

Cut all pieces in the order given unless otherwise instructed. For greater ease, instructions for cutting the appliqués are provided separately.

From the cream print, cut:
1 rectangle, 5" x 14"
1 rectangle, 4½" x 8½"
1 rectangle, 1½" x 4½"
8 squares, 1½" x 1½"
4 rectangles, 1½" x 2½"

From the red print, cut:
1 square, 2½" x 2½"
8 squares, 1½" x 1½"

Piecing and Appliquéing the Hospitality Hanger

Sew all pieces with right sides together using a ¼" seam allowance unless otherwise noted. Refer to "Invisible Machine Appliqué" on page 107 and "Wool Appliqué"

on page 115 for complete step-by-step instructions, or use your own favorite methods. Appliqué patterns are provided on page 49.

1. Using a pencil and an acrylic ruler, draw a diagonal sewing line from corner to corner on the wrong side of four cream 1½" squares and each red 1½" square.

2. Layer a prepared cream square over one corner of the red 2½" square. Stitch the pair together on the drawn line. Refer to "Pressing Triangle Units" on page 107 to fold, trim, and press the layers. In the same manner, stitch a prepared cream square to the remaining corners of the red square to make a square-in-a-square unit measuring 2½" square, including the seam allowances.

Make 1.

3. Layer a prepared red 1½" square onto one end of a cream 1½" x 2½" rectangle. Stitch, fold, press, and trim as instructed in step 2 to form a star point. In the same manner, stitch a second red square to the remaining end of the cream rectangle to form a mirror-image point. Repeat for a total of four flying-geese star-point units measuring 1½" x 2½", including the seam allowances.

Make 4.

4. Referring to the pictured hanger, lay out the step 2 and 3 units and the remaining four cream print squares in three horizontal rows to form the Star block. Join the pieces in each row. Press the seam allowances away from the star-point units and square-in-a-square unit. Join the rows. Press the seam allowances toward the top and bottom rows. The Star block should measure 4½" square, including the seam allowances.

5. Join the cream 4½" x 8½" rectangle to the top edge of the Star block and the cream 1½" x 4½" rectangle to the bottom edge of the Star block. Press the seam allowances toward the rectangles. The pieced hanger front should now measure 4½" x 13½", including the seam allowances.

YULETIDE STYLE

Gingerbread Cake with Vanilla Sauce

To me, nothing says Christmas quite like gingerbread. I've been baking this holiday treat for years, and the vanilla sauce is the icing on the cake . . . literally! For another great option, divide the batter between two or three mini loaf pans, and then drop the cooled loaves into cellophane bags for gifts.

~ Kim

Cake

1 cup sour cream (I use light)
½ cup packed brown sugar
1 egg
⅓ cup molasses
1½ cups flour
1 teaspoon *each* cinnamon, ginger, salt,
    and baking soda

Vanilla Sauce

½ cup (1 stick) butter
½ cup granulated sugar
½ cup packed brown sugar
½ cup heavy cream
⅛ teaspoon salt
Pinch of nutmeg (if desired)
2 teaspoons vanilla

Preheat oven to 350°F. In a medium bowl, use a mixer on medium speed to blend the first four cake ingredients. Add remaining cake ingredients and mix until blended. Pour batter into a greased and floured 9" pan, either square or round, and bake 30 to 40 minutes or until cake tests done with a toothpick.

While cake is baking, combine all sauce ingredients except vanilla in a small saucepan. Cook over medium heat, stirring occasionally, until the mixture comes to a boil; then remove from heat and add vanilla. The sauce will thicken as it cools. To serve, drizzle warm sauce over individual pieces of cake. Refrigerate any leftover sauce.

6. Using your favorite wool-appliqué method, cut and prepare the following wool appliqués:
- 1 pineapple from gold wool
- 9 leaves from assorted green wool scraps
- 5 large pennies from assorted wool scraps
- 5 small pennies from assorted wool scraps

7. Referring to "Making Bias-Tube Stems and Vines" on page 111, prepare the stem from the green rectangle. Apply a small amount of liquid fabric glue to the back of one end of the stem, fold the raw end over to the back approximately ¼", and heat set with a hot, dry iron.

8. Using the hanger pictured on page 46 as a guide, lay out and baste the appliqué design to the hanger front. Work from the bottom layer to the top to appliqué the pieces.

Completing the Hospitality Hanger

1. Layer the hanger top and batting (no backing is necessary). Quilt the layers. The featured hanger was hand quilted in the big-stitch method (see page 120) using the H212 Faded Brown perle cotton, with the star stitched in the ditch (along the seam lines) and the appliqués outlined to emphasize their shapes. A diagonal crosshatch was stitched onto the pineapple.

2. Trim away the excess batting. Referring to the pictured hanger and using the water-soluble marker, make a mark at the side and bottom edges 1¼" from each bottom corner. With the dots aligned at each corner, use a rotary cutter and an acrylic ruler to cut away the bottom hanger-top corners.

3. Pleat one end of the wired ribbon so that it measures approximately ½" wide; pin to the hanger front, approximately ¾" in from one top corner, with the hanger and ribbon raw edges flush. Repeat with the remaining top corner. Coil the ribbon lengths and pin them to the center of the hanger, positioning them away from the seam areas to be stitched. Center the hanger over the cream 5" x 14" rectangle, right sides together, and pin the layers together. Starting at one side edge and beginning and ending with a couple of back stitches, sew the layers together, leaving a 2½" to 3" opening for turning. Clip the fabric at the top corners. Trim away the excess fabric at the bottom corners.

4. Turn the hanger right sides out. Remove the pin from the ribbon, and lightly stuff the hanger with fiberfill. Use matching thread to hand stitch the opening closed. Use the ribbon to tie the hanger onto a doorknob (or anywhere you'd like), fluffing the finished bow and trimming the ends to the desired length at an angle.

Holly Door Hanger

Cutting

Cut all pieces in the order given unless otherwise instructed. For greater ease, instructions for cutting the appliqués are provided separately.

From the cream print, cut:
1 rectangle, 4½" x 13½"
1 rectangle, 5" x 14"

Appliquéing and Quilting the Holly Hanger

Sew all pieces with right sides together using a ¼" seam allowance unless otherwise noted. Refer to "Invisible Machine Appliqué" on page 107 and "Wool Appliqué" on page 115 for complete step-by-step instructions, or use your own favorite methods. Appliqué patterns are provided below.

1. Referring to the hanger pictured on page 48 for color choices, cut and prepare the following appliqués:
   - 10 leaves
   - 3 stars
   - 5 berries
2. Using an acrylic ruler, measure 1¼" from each bottom corner of the neutral 4½" x 13½" rectangle and mark a dot at the fabric side and bottom edges. Using the water-soluble marker, draw a diagonal line to connect the dots at each corner (these areas will be trimmed away later).

3. Referring to step 7 of "Piecing and Appliquéing the Hospitality Hanger" on page 48, stitch, prepare, and turn under one raw end of the green bias strip. Using the photo as a guide, lay out the stem, leaves, stars, and berries. Baste and stitch the stem and appliqués in place.

4. Layer the hanger top and batting (no backing is necessary). Quilt the layers. The featured hanger was hand quilted in the big-stitch method (see page 120), outlining the appliqués for emphasis. Stitch red buttons as desired to any open areas, knotting the thread on the hanger top wrong side. Trim away the excess batting. Trim the bottom corners on the marked lines.

Completing the Holly Hanger

Refer to steps 3 and 4 of "Completing the Hospitality Hanger" on page 48 to complete the hanger.

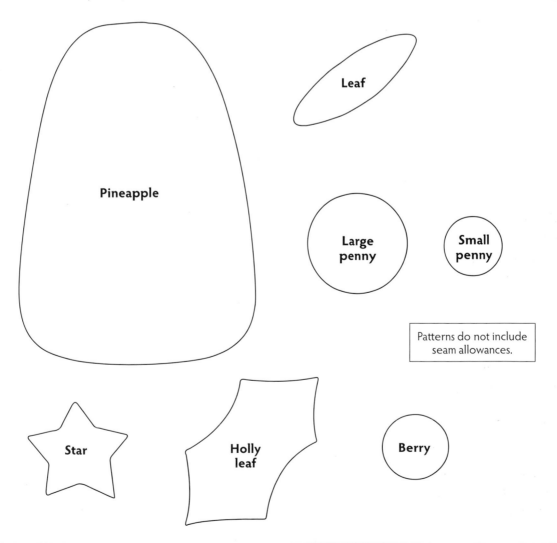

Leaf

Pineapple

Large penny

Small penny

Patterns do not include seam allowances.

Star

Holly leaf

Berry

Winter Delight Candle Mat

Perfectly sized to grace any nook or cranny of your home, this petite quilt features delightfully mingled sprays of winter greens, flowers, and plump, juicy berries. Best of all, with its classic red-and-green color scheme, this little quilt can be enjoyed throughout Christmas and beyond.

Materials

Yardage is based on 42" of useable fabric width after prewashing and removing selvages.

1 fat quarter (18" x 22") of dark-green print for appliqués, pieced border, and binding

4 chubby sixteenths (9" x 11") of assorted light-cream prints for center-block background

4 chubby sixteenths of assorted red prints for appliqués and pieced border

3 chubby sixteenths of assorted green prints for appliqués and pieced border

1 fat eighth (9" x 22") of medium-cream print for pieced border

1 fat eighth of red stripe for center block and pieced border

1 chubby sixteenth of green stripe for stems

1 charm square (5" x 5") of cream-and-red print for flower-center appliqués

⅔ yard of fabric for backing

23" x 23" square of batting

Supplies for your favorite appliqué method

Bias bar to make ⅜"-wide stems

Liquid glue for fabric, water soluble and acid free

Cutting

Cut all pieces across the width of the fabric in the order given unless otherwise noted. Refer to "Cutting Bias Strips" on page 105 to cut bias strips. Refer to "Invisible Machine Appliqué" on page 107 for complete step-by-step instructions, or use your own favorite method. Appliqué patterns are on page 57.

From *each* of the 4 assorted light-cream prints, cut:
1 square, 6½" x 6½" (combined total of 4)

From the green stripe, cut *on the bias*:
4 strips, 1¼" x 7"
4 strips, 1¼" x 4"

From the dark-green print, cut:
4 binding strips, 2½" x 22"
1 square, 1⅞" x 1⅞"; cut in half diagonally *once* to yield 2 triangles
Reserve the remainder of the print for the appliqués.

From the red stripe, cut:
4 squares, 1½" x 1½"
4 strips, 1½" x 12½"

From 1 red print, cut:
4 squares, 2½" x 2½"
1 square, 1⅞" x 1⅞"; cut in half diagonally *once* to yield 2 triangles
Reserve the remainder of the print for the appliqués.

From the 3 remaining assorted red prints and the 3 assorted green prints, cut a *combined total* of:
40 squares, 1½" x 1½"
6 squares, 1⅞" x 1⅞"; cut each square in half diagonally *once* to yield 12 triangles (I cut one from each print.)
Reserve the scraps of all the red and green prints for the appliqués.

From the reserved scraps of red and green prints, cut:
4 apple appliqués from one red print
4 apple-center appliqués from one green print
8 small leaf appliqués from assorted green prints
12 large leaf appliqués from assorted green prints
4 flower appliqués from two red prints (I cut two flowers from each of her two chosen prints.)
4 berry appliqués from one red print

From the cream-and-red print, cut:
4 flower-center appliqués

From the medium-cream print, cut:
20 rectangles, 1½" x 2½"
4 squares, 1⅞" x 1⅞"; cut each square in half diagonally *once* to yield 8 triangles

FINISHED QUILT SIZE: 16½" x 16½"
FINISHED CENTER BLOCK: 12" x 12"

Designed, pieced, and machine appliquéd by Kim Diehl.
Machine quilted by Deborah Poole.

YULETIDE STYLE

Raspberry Kiss Thumbprint Cookies

Years ago during a holiday baking binge, I went on a quest for the perfect thumbprint cookie. When I couldn't find exactly what I was envisioning, I adapted my Chocolate Chip Snowball Cookie recipe (page 30) and created my own version of this classic treat. The addition of the raspberry jam takes these completely over the top.

~ Kim

1 cup granulated sugar
½ cup (1 stick) butter, softened
4 ounces Neufchatel cheese or cream cheese
¼ cup sour cream (I use light)
2 eggs
1 teaspoon vanilla
¼ teaspoon almond extract
3½ cups plus 1 tablespoon flour
2 teaspoons baking powder
½ teaspoon baking soda
½ teaspoon salt
¼ cup seedless raspberry jam
1 bag (12 ounces) Hershey's Kisses
¼ cup additional granulated sugar for rolling

Remove wrappers from chocolate pieces. Preheat oven to 375°F. In a large mixer bowl, beat 1 cup sugar, butter, Neufchatel cheese, and sour cream on medium speed until fluffy. Beat in eggs, one at a time, until combined. Stir in vanilla and almond extract. In a separate bowl, combine the flour, baking powder, baking soda, and salt; add to wet mixture in two or three additions, beating well after each addition. Cover dough with plastic wrap and refrigerate one hour. Roll dough into walnut-sized balls, and then roll in granulated sugar to coat. Use your thumb or the back of a spoon to make a slight indentation in the top of each ball, and then fill with approximately ¼ teaspoon of raspberry jam. Bake on ungreased cookie sheets for approximately 10 minutes or just until set and very lightly browned on the bottom. While cookies are still warm, lightly press a Hershey's Kiss into center of each one. Makes approximately 3 dozen cookies.

Piecing and Appliquéing the Center Block

Sew all pieces with right sides together using a ¼" seam allowance unless otherwise noted.

1. Referring to "Making Bias-Tube Stems and Vines" on page 111, stitch and prepare the green-stripe 1¼" x 7" and 1¼" x 4" bias strips for stems.

2. With right sides together, fold each assorted light-cream 6½" square in half diagonally and use a hot, dry iron to press a center crease.

3. Dot the seam allowances of a prepared 7" stem with liquid fabric glue and press it onto the crease of a prepared light-cream square as shown. Heat set the stem from the square wrong side using a hot, dry iron. Repeat with the remaining 7" stems and light-cream 6½" squares.

Make 4.

4. Using a pencil and an acrylic ruler, draw a diagonal sewing line from corner to corner on the wrong side of each red-stripe and assorted red and green 1½" square.

5. Layer a prepared red-stripe 1½" square over one corner of a light-cream square from step 3. Stitch the pair together on the drawn line. Refer to "Pressing Triangle Units" on page 107 to fold, press, and trim the layers. Repeat with the remaining red-stripe and light-cream squares, taking care to position the striped fabric squares identically so they'll form a woven effect when the center block is pieced. Reserve the remaining prepared red and green squares for use in the inner border.

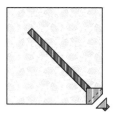

Make 4.

6. Referring to the quilt pictured on page 52, lay out the four cream squares from step 5 in two horizontal rows to form the center block. Join the squares in each row. Press the seam allowances of each row in opposite directions. Join the rows. Press the seam allowances open.

7. Position an apple appliqué onto the stem at each corner of the block, approximately ½" in from the block raw edges, ensuring the raw stem edge is overlapped at least ¼"; pin in place.

8. Position and pin a flower appliqué onto each side of the block approximately 1" in from the raw edge, centering it over the seam. Dot the seam of a prepared 4" stem with liquid fabric glue. Using the pictured quilt as a guide, tuck one end of the glue-basted stem under the 7" stem and curve the remaining length out to the flower, tucking the stem under the flower at least ¼". Repeat with the remaining sides of the quilt. Heat set the 4" stems from the block wrong side.

9. Position and baste three large leaves along each 7" stem. Position and baste two small leaves along each 4" curved stem. Remove the apple and flower appliqués. Use your favorite appliqué method to stitch the stem and leaf appliqués in place.

10. Reposition, baste, and stitch the apple and flower appliqués. Next, position, baste, and stitch the apple-center, flower-center, and berry appliqués. The pieced and appliquéd center block should measure 12½" square, including the seam allowances.

YULETIDE STYLE

Holiday Hostess Gift

During the holiday season, we look forward to rounds of parties, celebrations, and get-togethers with family and friends. Here's a unique and easy hostess gift to bring along. Wrap cinnamon sticks, whole cloves, and a thick-skinned orange into a large square of cellophane. Tie up the ends with a bow, attach a small tag giving instructions to simmer a slice of orange along with a small handful of the spices, and pair the package with a decorative teakettle (minus the whistling feature—you want to stay in your hostess's good graces!). This gift will keep on giving as it imparts moisture into dry winter air and lets the scent of Christmas waft all through the house.

Piecing and Adding the Borders

1. Layer a reserved prepared red or green square over one end of a medium-cream 1½" x 2½" rectangle. Stitch, fold, press, and trim as instructed in step 5 of "Piecing and Appliquéing the Center Block." In the same manner, layer, stitch, fold, press, and trim a second red or green print to form a mirror-image point. Repeat for a total of 20 flying-geese units, with the red and green prints used randomly.

Make 20.

2. Pair a medium-cream triangle and a dark-green or assorted red or green triangle; stitch the pair together along the long diagonal edges to make a half-square-triangle unit. Press the seam allowances toward the assorted print. Trim away the dog-ear points. Repeat to make one half-square-triangle unit from each of the prints for a total of eight half-square-triangle units. The remaining triangles will not be used.

Make 8.

3. Lay out five flying-geese units and two half-square-triangle units end to end to form a row. Join the pieces. Press the seam allowances open. Repeat for a total of four pieced strips.

Make 4.

4. Join a red-stripe 1½" x 12½" strip to the medium-cream side of a strip from step 3. Press the seam allowances toward the stripe. Repeat for a total of four pieced border strips.

Make 4.

5. Referring to the pictured quilt, join the red-and-green side of a pieced border strip to the right and left sides of the center block. Carefully press the seam allowances toward the center block.

6. Join a red 2½" square to each end of the remaining pieced border strips. Press the seam allowances toward the red squares. Join the red-and-green side of these strips to the remaining edges of the center square. Press the seam allowances toward the center square. The quilt top should now measure 16½" square, including the seam allowances.

Completing the Quilt

Layer the quilt top, batting, and backing. Quilt the layers. The featured quilt was machine quilted with an echo design in the center block background, and the appliqués were outlined to emphasize their shape. Arced lines were stitched onto the flying-geese units in the pieced border and straight lines were stitched at regular repeating intervals along the pattern of the striped fabric. An intersecting pumpkin-seed design was stitched onto the border corner squares. Join the four dark-green 2½" x 22" strips into one length and use it to bind the quilt.

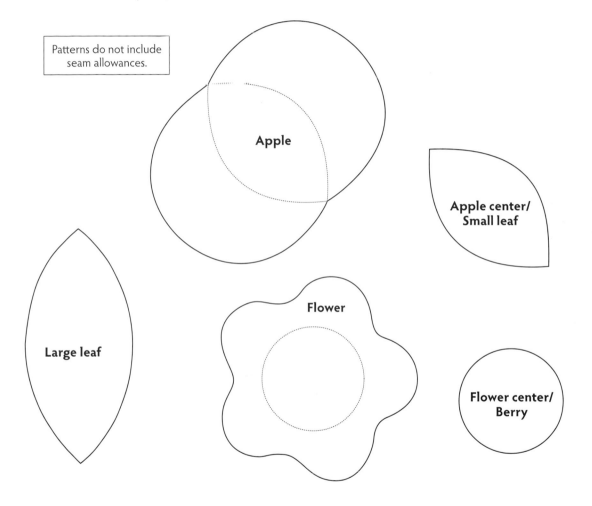

Patterns do not include seam allowances.

Apple

Apple center/ Small leaf

Large leaf

Flower

Flower center/ Berry

Christmas Baubles

This little trio of Christmas ornaments can be fashioned from scraps of fabric and wool gathered straight from your stash, and the ornaments work hand in hand to bring a touch of quaint and simple charm to your tree. But these baubles aren't just for your tree—try mingling them into your garlands, hanging them from doorknobs, or tying them to gift bags and packages for those special people in your life.

FINISHED ORNAMENT SIZES:
Penny Stack: 2½" x 2½" (excluding hanger)
Wooly Snowman: 3¼" x 5" (excluding hanger)
Scrappy Star: 4½" x 5" (excluding hanger)

Designed, pieced, and hand stitched by Kim Diehl.

Penny Stack Ornament

Materials

Materials will make 1 ornament.

3" x 3" square *each* of 2 wools for large penny front
    and back

2½" x 2½" square of wool for small penny

3" x 3" square of coordinating cotton print for yo-yo

½ yard of 1½"-wide wired ribbon for hanging tie
    (I chose deep cranberry red for contrast against
    the greenery of the tree)

Supplies for your favorite wool-appliqué method. If
    you're using my wool-appliqué method (page 115),
    you'll need a 6" x 6" square of paper-backed fusible
    web (I like HeatnBond Lite).

#8 or #12 black perle cotton

Size 5 embroidery needle

Liquid fabric glue, water soluble and acid free

Liquid seam sealant

Making the Ornament

Refer to "Wool Appliqué" on page 115 for complete step-by-step instructions, or use your own favorite method.

1. Using the patterns on page 67, prepare and cut two large pennies and one small penny from the wool squares.

2. Use the black perle cotton and embroidery needle to overhand stitch (see page 117) the small penny to the large penny chosen for the ornament front.

3. Use the yo-yo pattern to cut a circle from the coordinating cotton print. Refer to "Yo-Yos" on page 118 to make a yo-yo from the fabric circle.

4. Use the black perle cotton and the embroidery needle to sew the yo-yo to the penny unit from step 2 through the center opening, taking three or four stitches to secure it and leaving long thread tails. Knot the thread tails and trim them to the desired length.

5. Apply small dots of liquid fabric glue at approximately ½" intervals just inside the raw edge around the perimeter of the remaining large penny chosen for the ornament back. Lay it glue side up on a flat surface.

6. Trim the wired ribbon to approximately 14". Fold the ribbon in half crosswise to find the midpoint. Pleat the ribbon at the fold so that it measures approximately ½" wide. If needed, apply two or three dots of glue to the ribbon on the front and back near the fold. Sandwich the ribbon between

the penny front unit and the prepared penny back piece, with the fold resting approximately ¼" to ½" in from the penny edges. Anchor the ribbon from the front of the stack with a straight pin to keep it from shifting. Heat set the unit from the back to secure the ribbon and anchor the layers together.

7. Use the black perle cotton and embroidery needle, blanket stitch along the outer edges of the penny stack, securing the ribbon in place.

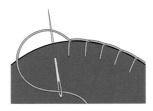

Blanket stitch

8. Remove the straight pin and use scissors to cut the ribbon ends at an angle. Apply a thin line of seam sealant to the ribbon ends to keep them from fraying; let dry. Tie the ornament to the tree using the ribbon ties, taking advantage of the wired edges to fluff and shape the lengths.

YULETIDE STYLE

Cinnamon Ornaments

When my daughters, Katie Pie and Molly Dolly, were little girls, we loved making cinnamon ornaments together at Christmastime. For even more fun, we took the "traditional" ornaments one step further and embellished them with whole cloves, making the house smell insanely delicious.

These ornaments are a snap to make. Mix 2 cups of applesauce, 3 cups of ground cinnamon, and 1 tablespoon of ground cloves. Roll the dough between sheets of waxed paper until it's a generous ¼" thick, and then cut out the shapes with cookie cutters. Use a straw or a skewer to poke holes for hanging, and then push in whole cloves to make special designs. Let the ornaments air-dry (usually two or three days), turning them occasionally so they'll dry evenly. String the finished ornaments with ribbon or raffia for hanging. Although this was a children's activity, I have to confess that mama loved it even more.

Wooly Snowman Ornament

Materials

Materials will make 1 ornament.

1 charm square *each* of 2 assorted beige wools for
    snowman
½" x 7" rectangle of wool for scarf
Scrap of orange cotton print for nose
Scrap of paper-backed fusible web
Fiberfill
5 buttons in assorted sizes and colors
#8 or #12 perle cotton in tan and black to stitch
    buttons and face
Size 5 embroidery needle
Freezer paper
14" of 19-gauge wire for hanger (easily found in any
    hardware store)
Needle-nose pliers with wire-cutting feature

YULETIDE STYLE

Holiday Treasure Boxes

If you're anything like me, your ornament collection continues to grow with each passing year—and there's only so much room on the tree! A neat way to display your treasures is to grab an empty container (a vintage box, basket, tin, or glass canister works beautifully), fill it with fresh or artificial evergreens, and nestle in your ornaments. Place these little treasure boxes in any available nook or cranny and enjoy Christmas all through the house!

Making the Ornament

1. Use a pencil to trace the snowman pattern on page 67 onto the dull, nonwaxy side of a piece of freezer paper, marking the opening where indicated. Place a second piece of freezer paper under the traced piece, waxy sides together, and use a hot, dry iron to fuse the layers. Cut out the snowman shape on the drawn lines.

2. Stack the two beige wool squares together, lay the freezer-paper snowman diagonally onto the stack, and pin it in place. Use scissors to cut out the snowman along the paper edges.

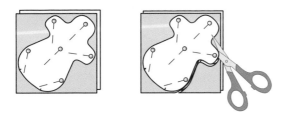

3. Remove the freezer-paper pattern. Use two straight pins to mark the position of the opening at the bottom and pin the remaining snowman edges to keep the pieces from shifting. Reduce the stitch length on your sewing machine (I reduced my stitch length from 2.2 to 1.8). Beginning and ending with two or three backstitches, use a ¼" seam allowance to machine stitch the snowman layers together, leaving an opening at the bottom for turning.

4. Clip each inner curve once, stopping two or three threads from the seam, and turn the snowman right side out. Lightly stuff with fiberfill, turn the fabric raw edges to the inside, and hand stitch the opening closed.

5. Use an awl or a straight pin to remove a couple of threads along each long side of the scarf, then repeat with each end, removing enough threads to form fringe. Tie the scarf around the snowman's neck. Use a needle and matching thread to sew a couple of stitches through the tie to anchor the scarf in place, burying the stitches within the wool to hide them. Knot and clip the thread under the scarf.

6. Trace the snowman nose onto the paper side of a piece of fusible web, and then use a hot, dry iron to press it to the wrong side of the orange scrap. Cut out the nose on the drawn line. Use the iron to fuse the nose onto the snowman face.

7. Referring to "Decorative Stitches" on page 118, use black perle cotton and the embroidery needle to stitch French knots to form the eyes and mouth. To end your stitching, bring the needle out through the back of the snowman underneath the scarf; knot and clip the thread.

8. Use tan perle cotton and the embroidery needle to attach the buttons to the front of the snowman body, knotting the thread on the front of the buttons and leaving decorative tails.

9. From the back of the snowman, gently poke one end of the wire through to the front of the arm, with about 1" or so of the wire exposed. Grab the very end of the wire with the needle-nose pliers, and then twist the pliers two or three times to coil the wire around the tip. Referring to the pictured ornament, form the remaining portion of wire into a curved shape to make the hanger, wrapping it here and there around a pencil to add little loops and curlicues. Insert the remaining end of the wire through the other arm, clip any excess length with the wire-cutting feature (if needed), and coil the end as previously instructed. To easily adapt this ornament to be hung on a doorknob, simply increase the length of the wire a bit.

PIN POINT

Snowman Faces

When stitching my snowman ornaments, I made each face look a little bit different so each one would have his own quirky look. I found that an easy way to audition the position of the eyes was to use glass-head pins, adjusting their placement until I was happy. As I stitched each eye, I removed the pin. Easy!

Scrappy Star Ornament

Anchor the center of the shape with a straight pin; use a rotary cutter and an acrylic ruler to cut out the pattern exactly on the drawn lines. Remove the pin and separate the layers to make six pattern pieces.

2. Using an iron on a hot, dry setting, fuse the pattern pieces, waxy sides down, to the wrong side of the six assorted rectangles. Use a rotary cutter and an acrylic ruler to cut out each star point, adding a ¼" seam allowance on all sides.

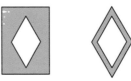

3. Pin two star points right sides together, with the pins placed in the fabric seam allowance. Reduce the stitch length on your sewing machine (I reduced my stitch length from 2.2 to 1.8). Stitch the pair together from fabric edge to fabric edge, exactly next to the paper. Repeat for a total of two joined pairs. Do not press the seams or remove the paper at this time.

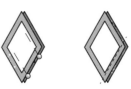

Materials

Materials will make 1 ornament.

2½" x 3½" rectangle *each* of 6 assorted prints for
    star points
6" x 7" rectangle of fabric for backing
¼ yard of ½"-wide ribbon (I used sheer gold organza)
Freezer paper
Fiberfill
1 small cream button
Size 5 embroidery needle
#8 or #12 perle cotton in a neutral color to stitch button

Making the Ornament

1. Use a pencil and an acrylic ruler to trace the star-point pattern on page 67 onto the dull, nonwaxy side of one end of a strip of freezer paper that's approximately 3" x 13". Accordion-fold the strip in widths to fit the pattern to produce six layers.

4. Referring to the illustration, pin and stitch a third star point to each joined pair to make two star halves. From the wrong side of each unit, with the paper still in place, press the seam allowances away from the center point. Finish pressing each unit from the front.

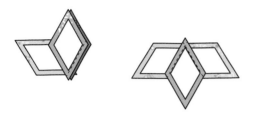

5. With right sides together, line up the center point of each unit; pin in place. Place a pin at each end of the layered halves. Stitch from fabric edge to fabric edge, exactly next to the paper. Press the center seam open from the wrong side, and then finish pressing from the front. Gently peel away the freezer paper.

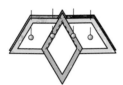

6. Stay stitch one seam at the inner V between two star points to reinforce it during the turning process. Layer the ends of the ribbon to form a loop and pin the ends to the center of the seam opposite the stay-stitched seam, with the side edges of the ribbon extending approximately ¼" beyond the star fabric. Stitch the ribbon in place, approximately ⅛" in from the inner V of the star point. Use a straight pin to anchor the ribbon loop to the center of the star, keeping it away from the edges.

7. With right sides together, layer the star and backing rectangle. Place a straight pin through each star point to anchor the unit securely to the backing. Use scissors to cut around the star, adding an approximate ⅛" seam allowance to the backing (just estimate this!).

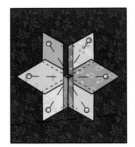

8. Starting at the inner point opposite the pinned ribbon, and beginning and ending with two or three backstitches, use a ¼" seam allowance to stitch around the star. Leave an unstitched area approximately ¼" long on each side of the stay-stitched seam for turning. Remove the pins.

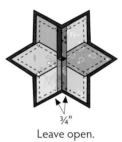

¾"
Leave open.

9. With the exception of the area left unstitched for turning, clip each inner point, stopping three or four threads from the seam line. Trim away the fabric at each outer point, a few threads away from the seam line. Carefully turn the star right side out, using the narrow end of a pen or a wooden skewer to push out the points, if needed.

10. Lightly stuff the star with fiberfill, turn the raw fabric edges to the inside, and hand stitch the opening closed. Use the neutral perle cotton and embroidery needle to add a button, stitching through all of the layers at the star center. Knot and clip the thread, leaving decorative tails.

YULETIDE STYLE

Ribbon Hangers for Glass Ornaments

When it comes to hanging glass ornaments on your tree, why use the traditional boring metal hooks that have been around for years? When I hang my glass ornaments, I slide 12" lengths of 1"- or 1½"-wide wired ribbon in assorted shades of red through the little metal loops at the top of the ornaments, cut the ribbon ends at an angle, and then tie them onto the tree (no bow needed!) before fluffing up the ribbon to make it look pretty. Spools of ribbon are frequently on sale in craft stores, so you can grab a couple of them in colors to suit your tree trimmings at a bargain price, and then pack them away for Christmas. This little trick adds an extra pop of color to your tree, and once you give it a try you'll throw your hooks away.

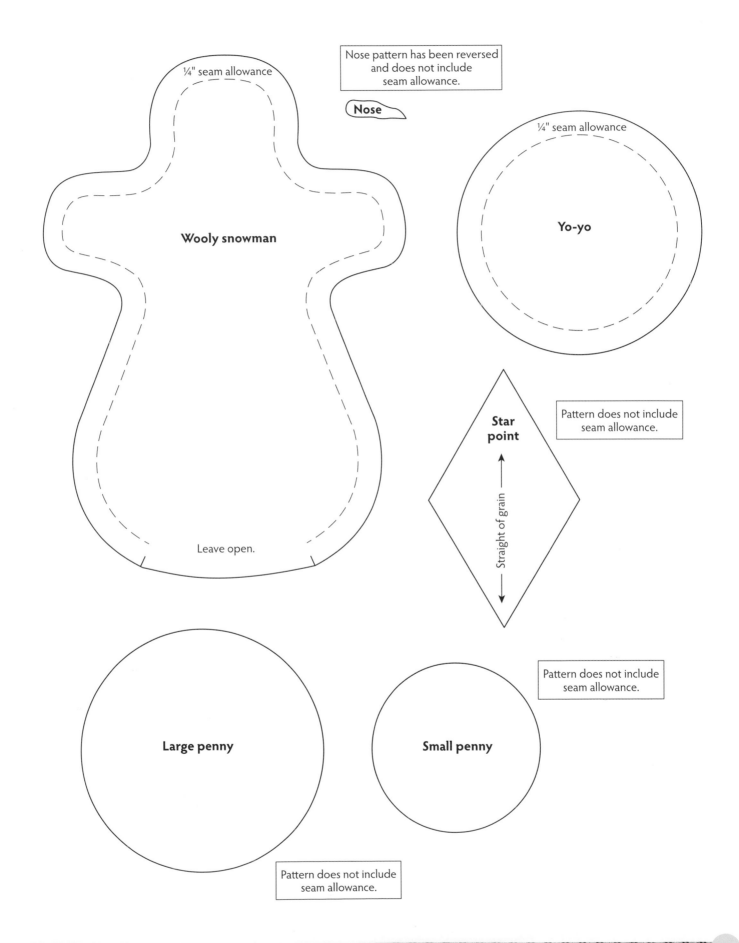

¼" seam allowance

Nose pattern has been reversed and does not include seam allowance.

Nose

¼" seam allowance

Wooly snowman

Yo-yo

Leave open.

Star point

Straight of grain

Pattern does not include seam allowance.

Large penny

Small penny

Pattern does not include seam allowance.

Pattern does not include seam allowance.

Holiday Hospitality Tree Skirt

This little quilt, with its classic star, pomegranate, and pineapple motifs, combines a variety of techniques into one fun-to-stitch project. Best of all, this quilt gives you options! Cut away the center and finish it as a tree skirt, or keep it as is for a fetching table topper.

Materials

Yardage is based on 42" of useable fabric width after prewashing and removing selvages.

2 yards of light print for blocks and appliqué backgrounds

⅔ yard of red print for patchwork and center opening binding and tie

½ yard of dark-green print for stems and outer binding

1 fat quarter (18" x 22") of gold print for patchwork

1 fat quarter of medium-green print for stems

7" x 8" rectangle *each* of 7 assorted green wools for leaf appliqués

7" x 7" square *each* of 5 assorted red wools for pomegranate and berry appliqués

6" x 6" square *each* of 4 assorted gold wools for pineapple appliqués

2" x 12" rectangle *each* of 4 assorted brown wools for vase appliqués

9" x 9" square of medium-blue wool for pomegranate centers

2⅔ yards of fabric for backing*

47" x 47" square of batting

Supplies for your favorite traditional- and wool-appliqué methods. If you're using my wool-appliqué method (page 115), you'll need approximately 1½ yards of 17"-wide paper-backed fusible web (I like HeatnBond Lite).

#8 or #12 perle cotton for stitching the wool (I used Valdani's #12 variegated perle cotton in H212 Faded Brown)

Green thread to stitch the vines

Size 5 embroidery needle

Size 9 straw needle

Bias bar to make ⅜"-wide stems

Liquid glue for fabric, water soluble and acid free

1" bias-tape maker

Water-soluble marker

*If you don't prewash your fabric and it has a selvage-to-selvage measurement of at least 44", you can reduce this amount to 1⅜ yards.

Cutting

Cut all pieces across the width of the fabric in the order given unless otherwise noted. Refer to "Cutting Bias Strips" on page 105 to cut the bias strips. For greater ease, cutting instructions for the wool appliqués are provided separately.

From the neutral print, cut:

6 strips, 1½" x 42"; crosscut into:
- 64 squares, 1½" x 1½"
- 32 rectangles, 1½" x 2½"
- 4 rectangles, 1½" x 10½"

1 strip, 10½" x 42"; crosscut into 1 square, 10½" x 10½". From the remainder of this strip, cut:
- 4 rectangles, 2½" x 4½"
- 10 rectangles, 3" x 5½"

4 strips, 3" x 42"; crosscut into:
- 6 rectangles, 3" x 5½"
- 32 squares, 3" x 3"

2 strips, 15½" x 42"; crosscut into 4 squares, 15½" x 15½"

From the gold print, cut:

8 squares, 2½" x 2½"

64 squares, 1½" x 1½"

Continued on page 71

FINISHED QUILT SIZE: 40½" x 40½"

Designed, pieced, and hand appliquéd by Kim Diehl.
Machine quilted by Deborah Poole with hand-quilted accents by Kim Diehl.

Continued from page 68

From the red print, cut:

1 strip, 5½" x 42"; crosscut into 4 squares, 5½" x 5½".
   From the remainder of this strip, cut 6 squares,
   3" x 3".

2 strips, 3" x 42"; crosscut into 26 squares, 3" x 3"

Enough 2"-wide *bias* strips to make a 34" length when
   joined end to end using straight, not diagonal,
   seams. (Please note that this strip will form
   the center opening binding and tie and will
   accommodate an opening of approximately 4"
   in diameter. If you opt to change the size of the
   opening, the length of the strip should be adjusted
   accordingly. Omit this cutting step if you choose to
   use the quilt as a table topper.)

From the dark-green print, cut:

5 binding strips, 2½" x 42"
4 rectangles, 1½" x 3"

From the medium-green print, cut:

16 *bias* strips, 1¼" x 9"

Piecing the Large and Small Star Blocks

*Sew all pieces with right sides together using a ¼" seam
allowance unless otherwise noted.*

1. Using a pencil and an acrylic ruler, draw a diagonal
   sewing line from corner to corner on the wrong
   side of 32 light 1½" squares, 16 neutral 3" squares,
   64 gold 1½" squares, and each red 3" square.

2. Layer a prepared light 3" square onto one corner of
   a red 5½" square. Stitch the pair together on the
   drawn line. Refer to "Pressing Triangle Units" on
   page 107 to fold, press, and trim the layers. In the
   same manner, stitch a prepared light 3" square to
   the remaining corners of the red square to make a
   square-in-a-square unit. Repeat for a total of four
   units measuring 5½" square, including the seam
   allowances.

Make 4.

3. Layer a prepared red 3" square onto one end of a
   light 3" x 5½" rectangle. Stitch, fold, press, and trim
   as instructed in step 2 to form a star point. In the
   same manner, layer, stitch, fold, press, and trim
   again with a second red 3" square to make a mirror-
   image point. Repeat for a total of 16 red flying-
   geese star-point units measuring 3" x 5½", including
   the seam allowances.

Make 16.

4. Lay out one square-in-a-square unit, four flying-
   geese star-point units, and four light 3" squares in
   three horizontal rows as shown. Join the pieces
   in each row. Press the seam allowances toward

the squares and square-in-a-square unit. Join the rows. Press the seam allowances away from the middle row. Repeat for a total of four large Star blocks measuring 10½" square, including the seam allowances.

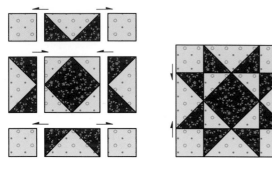

Make 4.

5. Repeat step 2 using the prepared light 1½" squares and gold 2½" squares to make eight square-in-a-square units. Repeat step 3 using the light 1½" x 2½" rectangles and gold 1½" squares to make 32 flying-geese star-point units. Refer to step 4 to lay out the pieced units with the neutral 1½" squares to make eight small Star blocks measuring 4½" square, including the seam allowances.

Piecing the Tree-Skirt Top

1. Lay out two small Star blocks, one large Star block, one neutral 2½" x 4½" rectangle, and one light 1½" x 10½" rectangle in three horizontal rows as shown. Join the blocks and rectangle in the top row. Press the seam allowances toward the rectangle. Join the rows. Press the seam allowances toward the light 1½" x 10½" rectangle. Repeat for a total of four star units measuring 10½" x 15½", including the seam allowances.

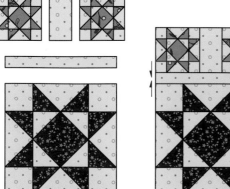

Make 4.

2. Join a neutral 15½" square to each long side of a star unit from step 1. Press the seam allowances toward the light squares. Repeat for a total of two rows measuring 15½" x 40½", including the seam allowances.

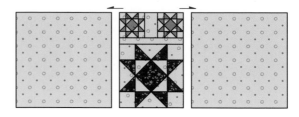

Make 2.

3. Join the small-star edges of the remaining two Star units to opposite sides of the light 10½" square. Press the seam allowances toward the light square. The middle row should measure 10½" x 40½", including the seam allowances.

4. Using the pictured quilt as a guide, join the step 2 rows to the step 3 middle row. Press the seam allowances away from the middle row. The pieced quilt top should now measure 40½" square, including the seam allowances.

Preparing and Stitching the Appliqués

Refer to "Wool Appliqué" on page 115 for complete step-by-step instructions, or use your own favorite method. Appliqué patterns are provided on page 75.

1. Referring to the quilt pictured on page 70 and using the colors indicated in "Materials" on page 68, prepare and cut the following wool appliqués:
   - 4 vases
   - 4 pineapples
   - 16 pomegranates
   - 16 pomegranate centers
   - 68 leaves
   - 32 berries

2. Referring to "Making Bias-Tube Stems and Vines" on page 111, stitch and prepare the dark-green print 1½" x 3 rectangles and the medium-green print 1¼" x 9" bias strips for use as stems and vines.

3. Use a ruler to measure 5" out from the seam of the middle row at each corner of the quilt top and use a water-soluble marker to make a small dot. Use a ruler and the marker to draw a diagonal line to connect the marks at each corner of the quilt top. These lines will serve as cutting guides when the corners of the quilt top are trimmed away after the appliqué design is stitched, and they will also be a helpful point of reference when laying out the appliqué design.

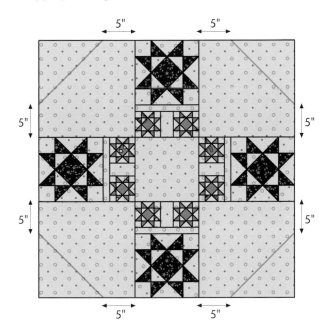

4. With right sides together, fold each corner of the quilt top in half. Use a hot, dry iron to lightly press a diagonal center crease from the inner corner of each light 15½" square to the outer corner.

5. Measuring 1" up from the drawn diagonal line on each light 15½" corner square, center a vase appliqué onto the background; pin in place. Dot the seam allowances of a prepared 3" stem with liquid fabric glue at approximately ½" intervals. Position the stem onto the background, tucking the raw end under the vase approximately ¼" and centering it over the background crease. Next, apply small dots of liquid fabric glue to the edges of the vase along the wrong side of the wool; reposition the vase on the background and use a hot, dry iron to heat set the pieces from the wrong side of the block.

6. Using the pictured quilt as a guide, glue baste and position a prepared pineapple to the background, approximately 2" up from the top of the vase,

centering it over the diagonal background crease and the stem and ensuring the stem is overlapped at least ¼". Glue baste, position, and heat set seven leaves to the background area above the pineapple as previously instructed.

7. Referring to the pictured quilt, position four pomegranate appliqués onto the background of the quilt-top corner; pin in place. Glue baste four prepared 9" vines with liquid fabric glue as previously instructed. Position each vine onto the background, tucking one raw end under the center stem and working out to position the opposite raw end under the pomegranate by at least ¼". (Any excess stem length can be trimmed away if desired.) Glue baste and reposition the pomegranates onto the background. Heat set the vines and pomegranates.

8. Using the pictured quilt as a guide, glue baste, position, and heat set 10 leaves and eight berries onto the background; add a center to each pomegranate to complete the design.

9. Use the straw needle and matching green thread to hand stitch the stem and vines, or use your own favorite appliqué method. After the stem and vines have been stitched, use the embroidery needle and perle cotton to stitch the wool appliqués.

10. Repeat steps 5–9 to add and stitch the appliqué design onto each corner of the quilt top.

Completing the Tree Skirt

1. Layer the quilt top, batting, and backing. Quilt the layers. The featured quilt was machine quilted with curved swags around the star centers and points, and the background areas were stitched with a stipple design interspersed with asterisk shapes to resemble snowflakes. The wool appliqués were outlined to emphasize their shapes, and for an added special touch, Kim used the same perle cotton used to stitch the wool appliqués to add a diagonal crosshatch onto the pineapples in the big-stitch style (see page 120).

2. *To finish this quilt for use as a table topper,* trim away the batting and backing along the quilt edges and the drawn lines at each corner. Join the strips of dark-green print into one length and use it to bind the quilt.

3. *To prepare the quilt for use as a tree skirt,* center a cup, bowl, or lid measuring approximately 4" in diameter onto the center of the quilted top; trace the circle shape using a water-soluble marker. (Please note that you can adjust the size of the center opening to be larger or smaller as needed to fit your Christmas tree.) Use a water-soluble marker and a ruler to draw a straight center line, extending it from the drawn circle through the patchwork to the outer edge of the quilt. Take a deep breath and cut away the center circle (you can do it!), continuing to cut along the drawn line to the quilt edge.

4. Trim away the batting and backing along the quilt edges and the drawn lines at each corner. Join the dark-green print strips to make one length and use it to bind the outer edges of the quilt, beginning and ending at the inner cut edges where they meet the circle. Trim away any excess green binding length to make the edges flush with the edges of the quilt top.

5. Following the manufacturer's instructions, use the bias-tape maker and the 2"-wide red strips to make a red print 1" x 34" bias strip. Turn the raw ends over to the folded side of the strip approximately ¼" and use your sewing machine threaded with matching thread to stitch the ends in place, approximately ⅛" in from the end. Fold the prepared strip in half lengthwise to enclose the long raw edges and the stitched raw ends within the strip; use a hot, dry iron to press the lengthwise fold along the strip.

6. Find and mark the midpoint of the binding strip by folding it in half and finger-pressing a center crease. Align the position of this crease with the midpoint of the circle opening opposite the straight cut edges. Pin the folded binding strip around the circle opening, with the raw circle edges encased within the folds of the binding; the binding length that extends beyond the tree skirt will form the ties. Beginning and ending at the tie ends, machine stitch the folded strip approximately ⅛" in from the edge, continuing along the quilt-center opening and ensuring that both the front and back folded edges are secured in place.

YULETIDE STYLE

Mulled Cider

When the snow is flying, what better way to stay toasty warm than with mulled cider? Here's my favorite recipe for this simple and scrumptious drink.
~ Kim

2 quarts apple cider
1½ teaspoons orange zest
½ teaspoon *each* whole allspice and ground coriander
1 generous teaspoon whole cloves
¼ teaspoon mace
⅛ teaspoon salt
1 generous tablespoon Red Hots (cinnamon candy)
3 sticks cinnamon, broken into large pieces

Pour cider into a kettle. Place remaining ingredients in a coffee filter and tie up with string. Bring cider to a slow boil, reduce the heat, and simmer 30 to 60 minutes to infuse the flavors. Ladle into mugs, sip, and enjoy!

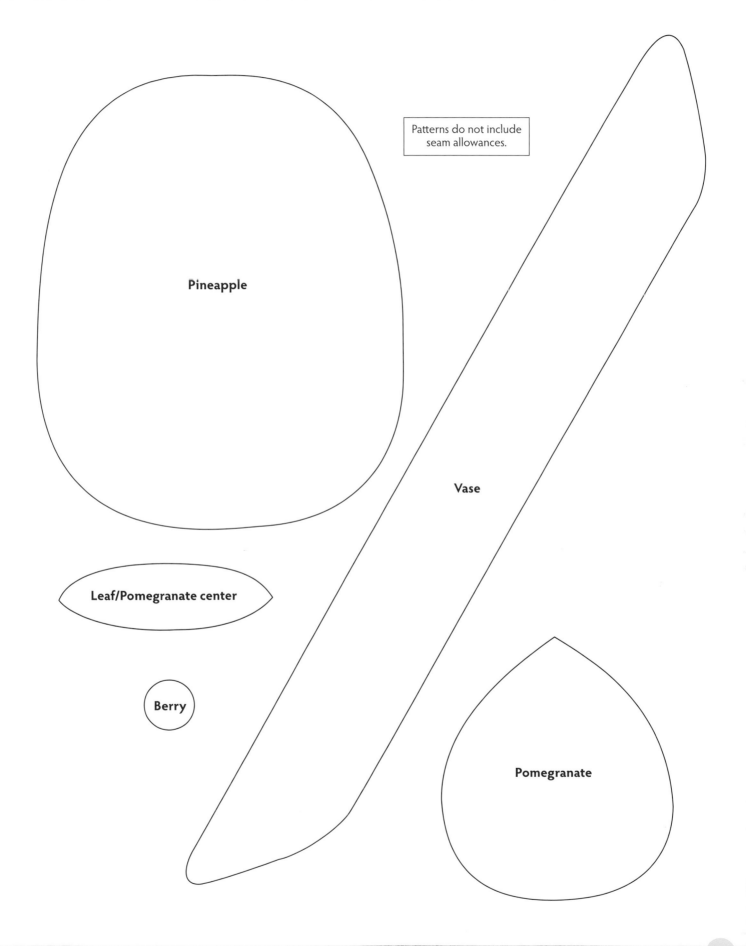

Patterns do not include seam allowances.

Pineapple

Vase

Leaf/Pomegranate center

Berry

Pomegranate

Scrap-Basket Stockings

Young or old, naughty or nice, we all love hanging our stockings by the chimney with care. Gather your favorite scrap-basket prints, pick a time-honored traditional pattern, and stitch up one of these little stockings for someone special.

FINISHED STOCKING SIZE:
5" x 15½" (excluding hanger)

Designed, pieced, and machine appliquéd by Kim Diehl. Machine quilted by Deborah Poole and Kim Diehl.

Basic Materials

The following materials are needed to make 1 stocking of any design. Additional materials for individual stocking designs are provided separately. Yardage for all stocking styles is based on 42" of useable fabric width after prewashing and removing selvages.

⅓ yard of print to coordinate with your chosen stocking design for cuff and lining

1 fat quarter (18" x 22") of coordinating print for stocking back and hanger

½ yard of muslin for stocking front and back backings

½ yard of batting

Freezer paper

Water-soluble marker

1" bias-tape maker

Basic Cutting

Cutting is for 1 stocking. For all stocking styles, cut all pieces across the width of the fabric in the order given unless otherwise noted. The cutting instructions that follow apply to all stocking designs. Additional cutting instructions for individual designs are provided separately. Using the freezer paper, refer to "Preparing Pattern Templates" on page 108 to make the stocking pattern provided on pages 88 and 89.

From the cuff and lining print, cut:

1 stocking*

1 reversed stocking*

1 rectangle, 6½" x 10½"

From the fat quarter of coordinating print, cut:

1 rectangle, 9½" x 17½"

1 rectangle, 2" x 5½"

*To cut the stocking and reversed stocking pieces at the same time, fold the fabric over to make a double thickness, pin the pattern in place, and cut out the pieces.

Basic Instructions

1. Follow the instructions for each individual stocking (beginning on page 79) to piece the stocking front.

2. Layer the pieced stocking front rectangle and the coordinating print 9½" x 17½" rectangle onto the batting and the muslin. Quilt the layers as desired.

3. Place the stocking pattern onto the right side of the quilted stocking front rectangle with the toe directed to the left, positioning it in a way that pleases you. Use the water-soluble marker to trace the stocking shape exactly along the pattern edges. Remove the pattern and machine stitch the entire stocking shape on the drawn line.

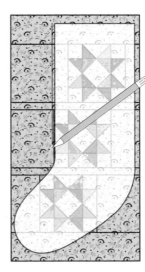
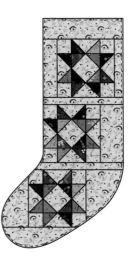

4. Layer the quilted stocking front over the quilted back piece, right sides together. Pin the layers along the inside edges of the stitched stocking outline, ensuring the pins don't cross the lines. Lay the pinned unit on a cutting mat and use a rotary cutter to cut out the front and back stocking pieces, following the line of stitching on the front piece.

5. Beginning and ending with a few backstitches, use a ¼" seam allowance to stitch the front and back pieces together, leaving the top edge of the stocking open. Turn the stocking right side out. (A long-handled wooden spoon works perfectly for this step.) Repeat to layer and join the stocking lining pieces, but do not turn right side out.

Leave open.

6. Place the stitched lining inside the pieced stocking, with the muslin side of the stocking facing the wrong side of the lining. You should see the "pretty" side of the lining when you look inside the stocking.

7. To make the hanging loop, lay the coordinating print 2" x 5½" strip on your ironing surface, wrong side up. Fold the long raw edges over to meet in the center; press. Fold the strip in half lengthwise to enclose the long raw edges. Use neutral or matching thread to machine stitch the long, open edges just inside the folds. Fold the strip in half, aligning the raw ends, and machine stitch a few threads in from the raw edges to form a loop.

8. With right sides together, join the narrow ends of the cuff 6½" x 10½" rectangle to form a tube. Press the seam allowances open. Fold the pieced tube in half, wrong sides together, keeping the seam aligned and the raw edges flush. Use a hot, dry iron to press the folded edge. Center the hanger over the cuff seam, aligning the raw edges, and stitch it in place.

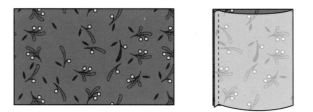

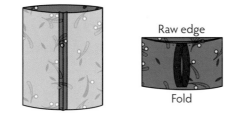

Raw edge

Fold

9. Insert the cuff into the stocking, aligning the raw edges and seams (the hanger should be positioned between the cuff and the lining); pin the top edges together. Machine stitch through all the layers along the top edge using a ¼" seam allowance. (I started stitching just before the hanger and stopped just after to overlap the stitching for added strength.) Fold the cuff to the outside of the stocking; the hanger will now be positioned approximately ¼" down from the top fold of the cuff. Press the top folded edge. The completed stocking should measure approximately 5" x 15½", excluding the hanger.

YULETIDE STYLE

Christmas Cashew Toffee

When the holidays roll around, this treat is the first thing my family asks for. When you begin munching on these little nuggets of crunchy goodness it's almost impossible to stop, so my best advice is to give in and enjoy it! And then break out your stretchy pants.

~ Kim

1 pound (4 sticks) salted butter (no substitute)
1½ cups granulated sugar
2 tablespoons water
1 cup lightly salted cashews, rough chopped
1 cup milk-chocolate chips
½ cup salted cashews, finely chopped, for topping

Combine the first three ingredients in a large nonstick skillet and cook over medium-high heat until a candy thermometer registers 315°F, stirring occasionally (this takes about 7 to 10 minutes). If you don't have a candy thermometer, the toffee should be done when it's the color of a brown paper bag. Turn off the heat and quickly stir in the chopped cashews; pour into a flexible, metal, nonstick 9" x 13" baking sheet with a rim. Let rest 2 or 3 minutes before sprinkling with milk-chocolate chips. After the chips are all melty, spread them over the toffee. Sprinkle with the finely chopped cashews. Refrigerate until cool and the chocolate is set, usually 2 to 3 hours. Flex the pan to pop the toffee out and break it into pieces.

Star Stocking

Materials

In addition to the basic materials (page 76), you'll also need the following.

⅓ yard of neutral print for stocking-front patchwork
1 charm square (5" x 5") *each* of 10 assorted prints for stocking-front patchwork

Cutting

In addition to the basic pieces (page 76), cut the following.

From the light print, cut:
1 strip, 4½" x 42"; crosscut into:
- 1 square, 4½" x 4½"
- 2 rectangles, 3½" x 4½"
- 2 rectangles, 2½" x 4½"
- 1 rectangle, 1½" x 4½"
1 strip, 2½" x 42"; crosscut into:
- 2 rectangles, 2½" x 9½"
- 3 squares, 2½" x 2½"
2 strips, 1½" x 42"; crosscut into:
- 12 rectangles, 1½" x 2½"
- 12 squares, 1½" x 1½"
2 rectangles, 1" x 9½"

From *each* of the 10 assorted-print charm squares, cut:
4 squares, 1½" x 1½" (combined total of 40)

Making the Stocking

Sew all pieces with right sides together using a ¼" seam allowance unless otherwise noted.

1. Using a pencil and an acrylic ruler, draw a diagonal sewing line from corner to corner on the wrong side of each print 1½" square.

2. Layer a prepared assorted 1½" square onto one corner of a light 2½" square. Stitch the pair together on the drawn line. Refer to "Pressing Triangle Units" on page 107 to fold, press, and trim the layers. In the same manner, stitch a prepared print square to the remaining corners of the light square to make a square-in-a-square unit. Repeat for a total of three square-in-a-square units measuring 2½" square, including the seam allowances.

Make 3.

3. Layer a prepared print 1½" square onto one end of a light 1½" x 2½" rectangle. Stitch, fold, press, and trim as instructed in step 1 to form a star point. In the same manner, stitch a second prepared print square onto the remaining end of the rectangle to form a mirror-image point. Repeat for a total of 12 flying-geese star-point units measuring 1½" x 2½", including the seam allowances. Please note that you'll have four unused assorted-print 1½" squares; these have been included for added versatility as you stitch the patchwork.

Make 12.

4. Lay out one square-in-a-square unit, four star-point units, and four light 1½" squares in three horizontal rows as shown. Join the pieces in each row. Press the seam allowances away from the star-point units. Join the rows. Press the seam

allowances toward the top and bottom rows. Repeat for a total of three Star blocks measuring 4½" square, including the seam allowances.

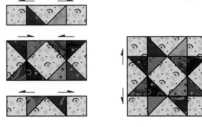

Make 3.

5. Lay out the Star blocks and the light background pieces in seven horizontal rows as shown. Join the pieces in each block row. Press the seam allowances away from the blocks. Join the rows. Press the seam allowances away from the block rows. The pieced stocking front unit should measure 9½" x 17½", including the seam allowances.

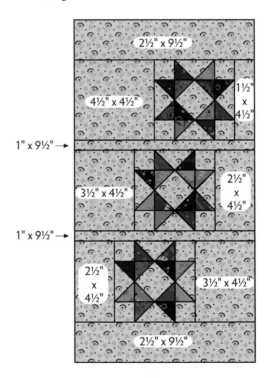

6. Refer to "Basic Instructions" on page 76 to finish the stocking.

Snowball Stocking

Materials

In addition to the basic materials (page 76), you'll also need the following.

3½" x 3½" square *each* of 17 assorted dark prints for stocking-front patchwork

1 charm square (5" x 5") *each* of 6 assorted light prints for stocking-front patchwork

1 chubby sixteenth (9" x 11") of light print for stocking-front patchwork

Cutting

In addition to the basic pieces (page 76), cut the following.

From the light chubby sixteenth, cut:
1 rectangle, 2½" x 9½"
14 squares, 1½" x 1½"

From *each* of the 6 assorted light charm squares, cut:
9 squares, 1½" x 1½" (combined total of 54)

Making the Stocking

1. Using a pencil and an acrylic ruler, draw a diagonal sewing line from corner to corner on the wrong side of the 68 light 1½" squares.

2. Referring to step 2 of "Star Stocking" on page 80, use the prepared light squares and dark 3½" squares to make 17 Snowball blocks measuring 3½" square, including the seam allowances.

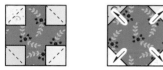

Make 17.

3. Lay out the Snowball blocks in three horizontal rows of three blocks each and two horizontal rows of four blocks each as shown. Join the blocks in each row. Press the seam allowances of each row in alternating directions so the seams will nest together. Join the rows. Press the seam allowances open. Join the light 2½" x 9½" rectangle to the top of the unit. Press the seam allowances toward the rectangle. The pieced stocking front unit should measure 12½" x 17½", including the seam allowances, at the widest and longest points.

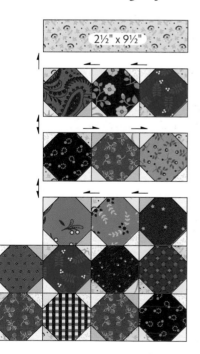

4. Refer to "Basic Instructions" on page 76 to finish the stocking.

Irish Chain Stocking

Materials

In addition to the basic materials (page 76), you'll also need the following.

1 charm square (5" x 5") *each* of 10 assorted prints for stocking-front patchwork

1 chubby sixteenth (9" x 11") *each* of 3 assorted light prints for stocking-front patchwork

1 fat eighth (9" x 22") of a different light print for stocking-front patchwork

Cutting

In addition to the basic pieces (page 76), cut the following.

From *each* of the 10 assorted charm squares, cut:
5 squares, 1½" x 1½" (combined total of 50)

From the light fat eighth, cut:
1 rectangle, 2½" x 9½"
Reserve the remainder of the print.

From *each* of the 3 light chubby sixteenths and the remainder of the light print fat eighth, cut:
10 squares, 1½" x 1½" (combined total of 40)
6 rectangles, 1½" x 3½" (combined total of 24)

Making the Stocking

1. Select five assorted 1½" squares and four assorted light 1½" squares. Lay out the pieces in three horizontal rows as shown to form a Nine Patch block. Join the squares in each row. Press the seam allowances toward the print squares. Join the rows. Press the seam allowances away from the middle row. Repeat for a total of eight Nine Patch blocks measuring 3½" square, including the seam allowances.

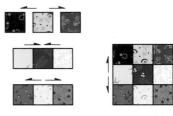

Nine Patch block.
Make 8.

2. Select three assorted light 1½" x 3½" rectangles. Join the pieces along the long edges as shown. Press the seam allowances toward the middle row. Repeat for a total of six Rail Fence A blocks measuring 3½" square, including the seam allowances.

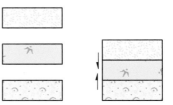

Rail Fence A block.
Make 6.

3. Select two light 1½" x 3½" rectangles, two light 1½" squares, and one print 1½" square (I used a different red print for each center square). Join a light square to each opposite side of the print square. Press the seam allowances toward the print square. Lay out the unit and the two light rectangles in three horizontal rows as shown on page 83. Join the rows. Press the seam allowances toward the middle row. Repeat for a total of three Rail Fence B blocks measuring 3½" square, including the seam allowances. You'll have seven

unused print squares and two unused light squares; these have been included for variety.

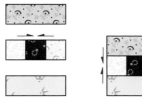

Rail Fence B block.
Make 3.

4. Lay out the blocks in three horizontal rows of three blocks each and two horizontal rows of four blocks each as shown. Join the blocks in each row. Press the seam allowances away from the Nine Patch blocks. Join the rows. Press the seam allowances open. Join the light 2½" x 9½" rectangle to the top of the unit. Press the seam allowances toward the rectangle. The pieced stocking front unit should measure 12½" x 17½", including the seam allowances, at the widest and longest points.

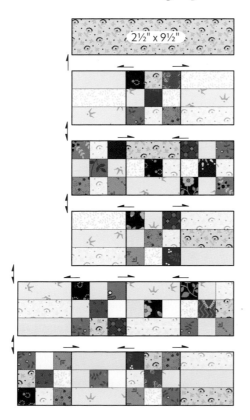

2½" x 9½"

5. Refer to "Basic Instructions" on page 76 to finish the stocking.

YULETIDE STYLE

Clove Oranges

Each year when the Christmas season arrives, one of my favorite traditions is making clove oranges for my table centerpiece. These are easy to make, and all you need are thick-skinned oranges and whole cloves. Use a toothpick (or grab an awl from your sewing room) to poke a pattern into the skin of the orange. Be liberal with your design, because the more cloves you use, the better preserved the orange will be and the scent will be heavenly. Next, push in the cloves. That's it! I place these oranges into bowls of evergreens and pomegranates for a beautiful burst of color, or arrange them onto trays, making sure to turn them every so often to keep them fresh. These look really pretty, and smell even better!

Chevron Stocking

Materials

In addition to the basic materials (page 76), you'll also need the following.

1 fat quarter (18" x 22") of light print for stocking-front patchwork

1 charm square (5" x 5") *each* of 13 assorted prints for stocking-front patchwork

Cutting

In addition to the basic pieces (page 76), cut the following.

From *each* of the 13 assorted print charm squares, cut:

4 squares, 1½" x 1½" (combined total of 52)
Reserve the remainder of the prints.

From the remainder of your 4 favorite assorted print charm squares, cut a *combined total of*:

4 squares, 1⅞" x 1⅞"; cut each square in half diagonally *once* to yield 2 triangles (combined total of 8)

From the light-print fat quarter, cut:

1 rectangle, 4½" x 9½"
1 rectangle, 2½" x 9½"
26 rectangles, 1½" x 2½"
4 squares, 1⅞" x 1⅞"; cut each square in half diagonally *once* to yield 2 triangles (combined total of 8)
3 squares, 2½" x 2½"
3 rectangles, 1½" x 9½"

Making the Stocking

1. Using a pencil and an acrylic ruler, draw a diagonal sewing line from corner to corner on the wrong side each print 1½" square.

2. Referring to step 3 of "Star Stocking" on page 80 and using the light 1½" x 2½" rectangles and the prepared print squares, make 26 flying-geese star-point units measuring 1½" x 2½", including the seam allowances.

Make 26.

3. Join a light and assorted 1⅞" triangle along the long diagonal edges to make a half-square-triangle unit. Press the seam allowances toward the print. Trim away the dog-ear points. Repeat for a total of eight half-square-triangle units measuring 1½" square, including the seam allowances.

Make 8.

4. Lay out six star-point units and two half-square-triangles in two horizontal rows as shown. Join the pieces in each row. Press the seam allowances open. Join the rows. Press the seam allowances open. Join a light 2½" square to the left side of the unit. Press the seam allowances toward the square. Repeat for a total of three short chevron rows. In the same manner, use the remaining eight star-point units

and two half-square-triangle units to piece one long chevron row.

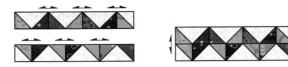

Short chevron row.
Make 3.

Long chevron row.
Make 1.

5. Lay out the short and long chevron rows, the three light 1½" x 9½" rectangles, the light 4½" x 9½" rectangle, and the light 2½" x 9½" rectangle in nine horizontal rows as shown. Join the rows. Press the seam allowances toward the light rectangles. The pieced stocking front should measure 9½" x 17½", including the seam allowances.

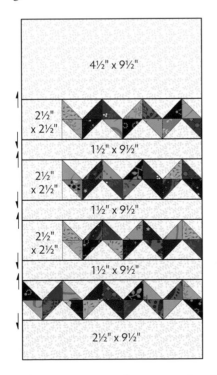

6. Refer to "Basic Instructions" on page 76 to finish the stocking.

Yo-Yo Stocking

Materials

In addition to the basic materials (page 76), you'll also need the following.

1 fat quarter (18" x 22") of light print for stocking-front background
1 charm square (5" x 5") *each* of 22 assorted prints for yo-yos
#8 or #12 perle cotton in a neutral color
Size 5 embroidery needle
Liquid glue for fabric, water soluble and acid free
Basting spray
Supplies for your favorite appliqué method

Cutting

In addition to the basic pieces (page 76), cut the following. The yo-yo pattern is on page 87.

From the light print, cut:
1 rectangle, 9½" x 17½"

From *each* of the 22 assorted print charm squares, cut:
1 yo-yo (combined total of 22)

Making the Stocking

1. Referring to "Yo-Yos" on page 118, make 22 yo-yos from the assorted-print circles. Please note that for the featured stocking, I cut one stitched yo-yo into two portions (later in the stocking process), using each half where only a partial yo-yo was needed. If you choose to use two different yo-yos, rather than one divided yo-yo, increase your charm square and yo-yo count to 23.

2. Center the stocking pattern onto the light 9½" x 17½" rectangle; use a pencil or water-soluble marker to trace exactly along the stocking-pattern edges. Lay an acrylic ruler over the top of the stocking so that the edge is resting 2½" down from the marked top. Using the illustration as a guide, lay out three yo-yos across the stocking, with the top edges just resting against the ruler and the outside edges of the outer yo-yos just resting approximately on or just beyond the drawn stocking lines. Lay out three additional rows of three yo-yos beneath the top row.

3. Lay out the remaining yo-yo rows to fill the foot area, keeping them in fairly close vertical alignment. Depending upon your yo-yo placement, you'll likely have two or three open areas near the heel and approximately midway along the top and bottom foot area. To fill these openings and keep the bulk of the gathered yo-yo centers from landing on the stocking edges where the pieces will be seamed, I chose two yo-yos and used my sewing machine to slowly stitch across the pieces just on each side of the gathered centers. I then used scissors to cut each yo-yo in half through the centers, trimming away any bulk at the gathered area. After repositioning the yo-yo halves to fill the open areas, use approximately six to eight drops of liquid fabric glue on the wrong side of each intact yo-yo and three or four dots on the yo-yo halves to anchor them in place within the stocking shape. From the front of the piece, use a hot, dry iron to press the yo-yos and flatten them slightly. From the back of the piece, heat set the glue-basted areas of the yo-yos to firmly attach them for stitching.

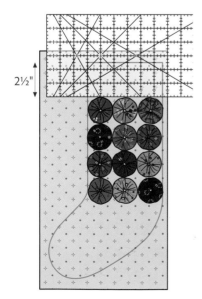

2½"

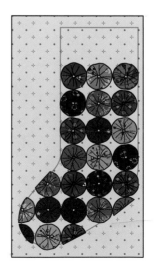

4. Layer the prepared yo-yo stocking front with the batting and muslin backing. Referring to "Invisible Machine Appliqué" on page 107, appliqué the yo-yos to the background, stitching through all layers to simultaneously appliqué and quilt the layers. Machine stitch the entire stocking shape on the drawn line, stitching slowly over the yo-yo edges where they extend beyond the stocking outline.

5. Referring to "Basic Instructions" on page 76, follow step 2 to quilt the stocking back pieces and steps 4–9 to finish the stocking.

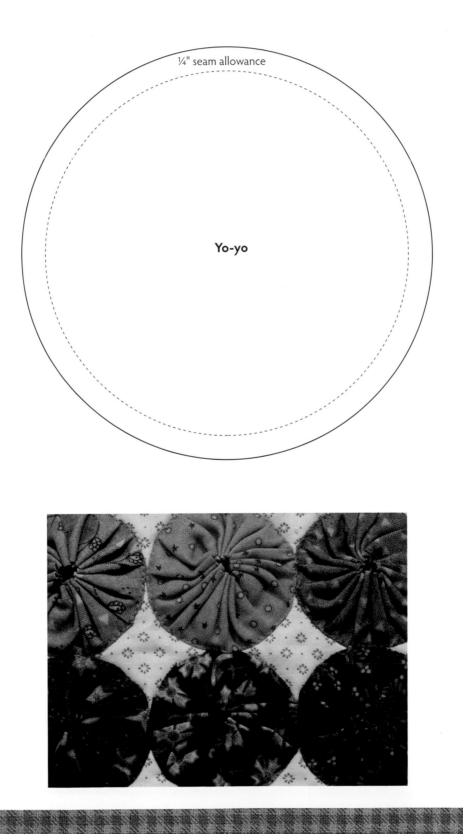

¼" seam allowance

Yo-yo

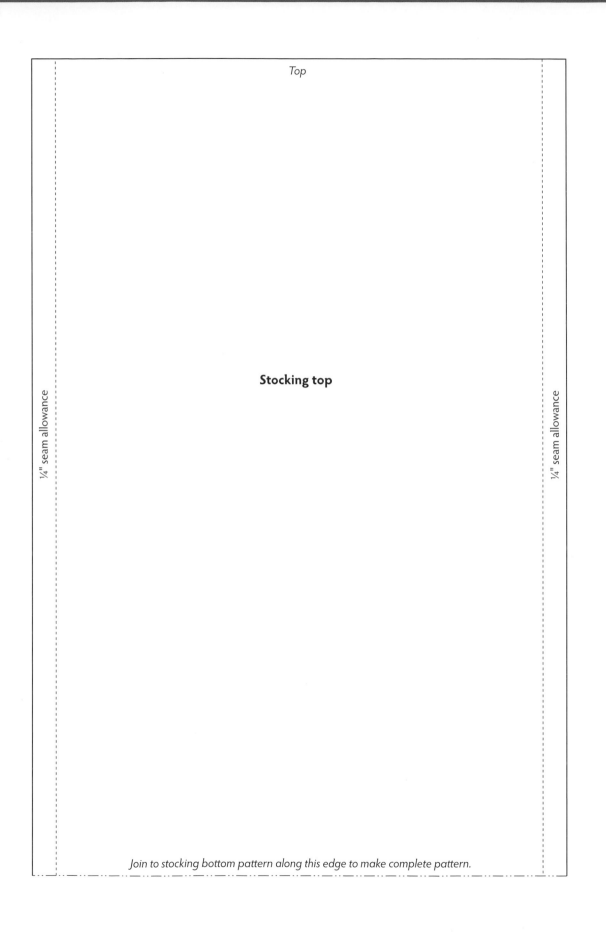

Top

Stocking top

¼" seam allowance

¼" seam allowance

Join to stocking bottom pattern along this edge to make complete pattern.

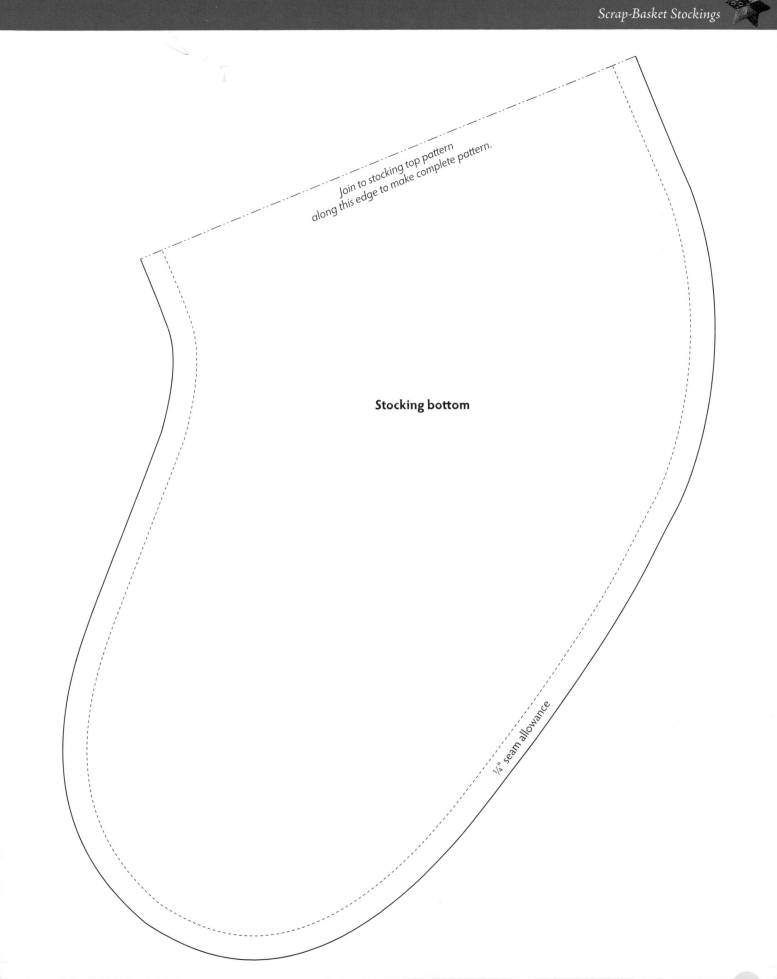

Join to stocking top pattern
along this edge to make complete pattern.

Stocking bottom

¼" seam allowance

Button Blizzard Pillow

What does a snowman do when it's wintry and cloudy with a good chance of…buttons? He grabs his warm woolies, bundles up, and tips his head to the sky to watch the "snow" fly.

FINISHED PILLOW SIZE: 14" x 14"

Designed, pieced, and hand appliquéd by Kim Diehl.
Machine quilted by Deborah Poole.

Materials

16" x 16" square of black print for pillow front
15" x 15" square of coordinating black print for
    pillow back
12" x 12" square of cream or beige wool for snowman
5" x 12" rectangle of medium-blue wool for scarf front
6" x 6" square of dark-blue wool for scarf back
3" x 6" rectangle of orange wool for carrot nose
20" x 20" square of muslin or light print for pillow-
    front backing
20" x 20" square of batting
Supplies for your favorite wool-appliqué method. If
    you're using my wool-appliqué method (page 115),
    you'll need approximately ½ yard of 17"-wide
    paper-backed fusible web (I like HeatnBondLite).
#8 or #12 perle cotton in black for the snowman eyes
    and a neutral color for stitching the wool appliqué
    (I used Valdani's #12 variegated perle cotton in
    H212 Faded Brown)
Size 5 embroidery needle
2½ yards of red jumbo (⅝"-wide) rickrack for pillow trim
Clear buttons in assorted sizes for snowflakes
4 assorted dark buttons for snowman front
Fiberfill

Quilting the Pillow Front

Layer the 16"-square pillow front with the 20"-square batting and backing pieces. Quilt the layers. For the featured project, the pillow front was machine quilted with a 1"-square grid using black thread to add subtle texture. Use a rotary cutter and an acrylic ruler to trim the quilted square to 14½" x 14½".

Preparing and Stitching the Wool Appliques

Refer to "Wool Appliqué" on page 115 for complete step-by-step instructions, or use your own favorite method. Appliqué patterns are provided on pages 93–95. Remember that for any nonsymmetrical pattern, the wool-appliqué method featured in this book will produce a finished shape that is reversed from the pattern provided; for greater ease, all patterns in this project have been reversed. Note that for the snowman pattern, it isn't necessary to add seam allowances or appliqué the straight side and bottom edges; they'll be enclosed within the seams of the finished pillow.

1. Cut and prepare one each of the wool appliqués indicated in "Materials" at left.

2. Using the pictured pillow on page 91 as a guide, lay out the appliqués on the pillow front, aligning the bottom-right corner edges of the snowman with the bottom-right corner of the quilted pillow front and ensuring that the raw edge of the scarf back piece is tucked under the snowman approximately ¼". Working from the bottom layer to the top, use the embroidery needle and perle cotton to stitch the appliqués in place.

3. Referring to the French knot illustration on page 118, use the black perle cotton to stitch two eyes. (I increased the number of wraps to five to make the eyes larger.)

4. Beginning at the bottom edge, 4" or 5" in from the corner, lay out and pin the rickrack along the pillow-front edges, with the inner curves of the outer rickrack edge resting approximately ⅛" in

from the pillow raw edge. Overlap the ends of the rickrack slightly, with the raw edges extending beyond the pillow edge. Machine stitch the rickrack in place and trim the raw rickrack ends flush with the pillow.

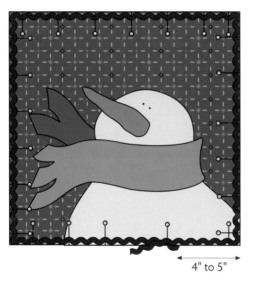

4" to 5"

5. Referring to the photo, use a needle and thread to stitch the buttons to the pillow front, knotting and clipping the thread tails on the wrong side so they'll be hidden.

6. Center the pillow front over the 15"-square pillow back, right sides together; pin the edges. Starting near the middle of one side edge, use a ¼" seam allowance to stitch the pieces together, leaving a 3" to 4" opening for turning the pillow.

7. Clip the corners and turn the pillow right side out. Lightly stuff with fiberfill, turn the raw fabric edges to the inside, and hand stitch the opening.

YULETIDE STYLE

Towel Time!

Because of their versatility, one of my favorite "go-to" items is purchased 20" x 28" kitchen towels. It's a snap to use cotton prints and your favorite fusible appliqué method to stitch a chubby snowman onto a towel corner and . . . voilà, instant Christmas gift! One of my Martingale friends, Karen Soltys, also gave me the most fabulous idea for adding wooly snowmen to opposite towel corners, and of course I couldn't resist. For added color, I used a small lid and buttons to create penny "snowflake" patterns from my wool scraps, stitching them randomly onto the towel and hiding my knots between the layers. No backing piece was needed, and I love that this wintry table topper can be used until the spring thaw!

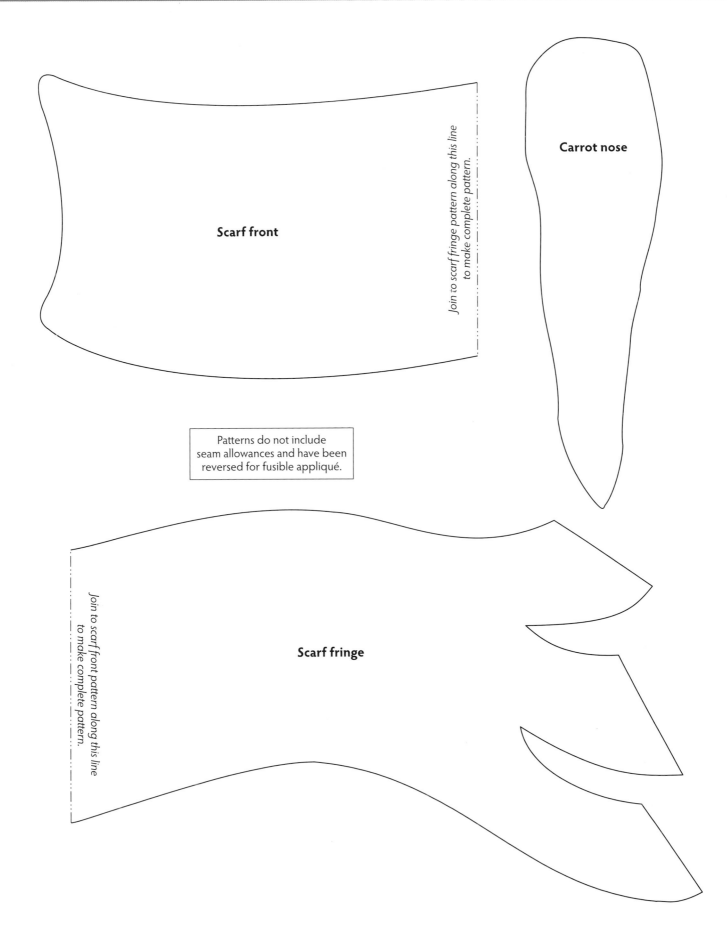

Carrot nose

Scarf front

Join to scarf fringe pattern along this line to make complete pattern.

Patterns do not include seam allowances and have been reversed for fusible appliqué.

Scarf fringe

Join to scarf front pattern along this line to make complete pattern.

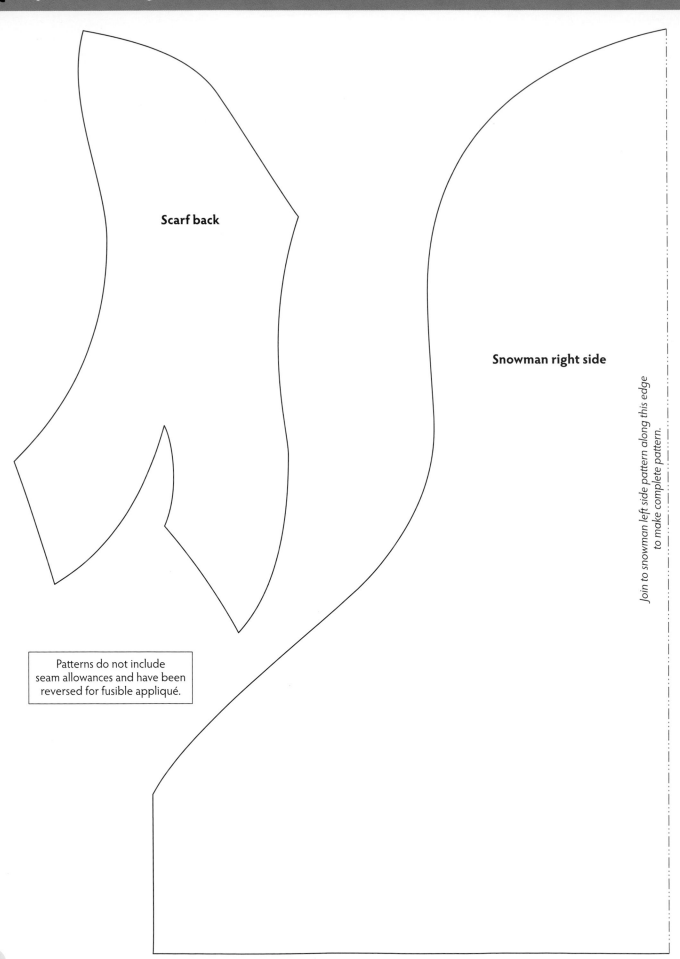

Scarf back

Snowman right side

Join to snowman left side pattern along this edge to make complete pattern.

Patterns do not include seam allowances and have been reversed for fusible appliqué.

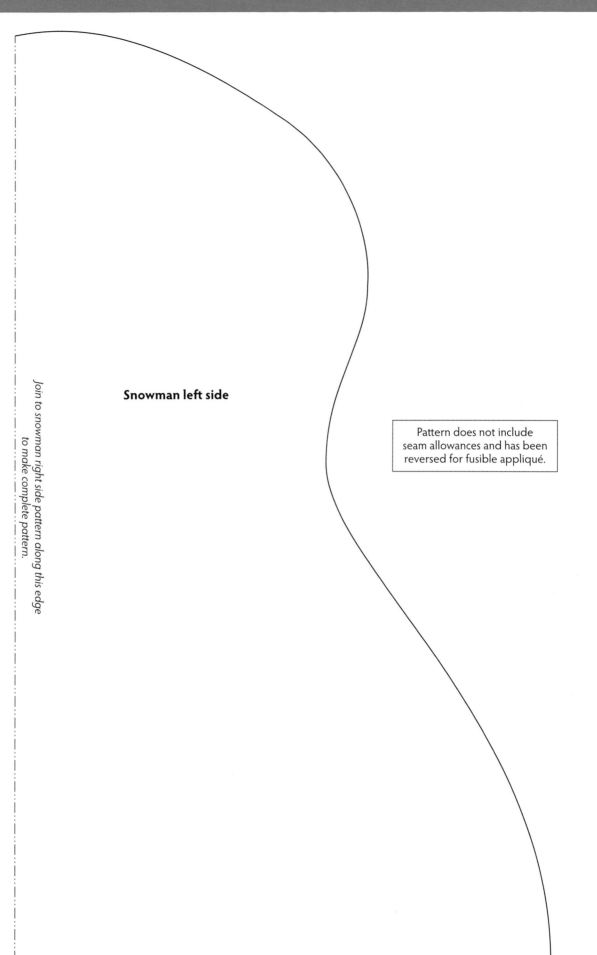

Snowman left side

Join to snowman right side pattern along this edge to make complete pattern.

Pattern does not include seam allowances and has been reversed for fusible appliqué.

Yuletide Cheer Lap Quilt

Patchwork boughs of evergreens, twinkling stars, and a flock of Christmas geese capture all the magic of the holiday season. Wrap someone you love within the folds of this colorful quilt, and they're sure to be wreathed in smiles.

Materials

Yardage is based on 42" of useable fabric width after prewashing and removing selvages.

2⅞ yards of tan print for blocks, sashing, and outer border

1 fat eighth (9" x 22") *each* of 16 assorted prints (I chose red, blue, gold, orange, and brown prints) for stars and outer border

⅓ yard *each* of 6 assorted green prints for blocks and outer border

1 yard of dark-brown print for inner border and binding

¼ yard (not a fat quarter) of red print #1 for blocks and outer-border corner squares

1 fat quarter (18" x 22") of red print #2 for blocks

1 fat quarter of dark-red print for blocks

3¾ yards of fabric for backing

67" x 67" square of batting

Cutting

Cut all pieces across the width of the fabric in the order given unless otherwise noted.

From the tan print, cut:
17 strips, 1½" x 42"; crosscut into:
- 100 squares, 1½" x 1½"
- 208 rectangles, 1½" x 2½"
8 strips, 3½" x 42"; crosscut into:
- 36 squares, 3½" x 3½"
- 12 rectangles, 3½" x 10½"
16 strips, 2½" x 42"; crosscut into:
- 12 rectangles, 2½" x 10½"
- 192 squares, 2½" x 2½"

From *each* of the 6 assorted green prints, cut:
12 rectangles, 1½" x 5½" (combined total of 72)
12 rectangles, 1½" x 3½" (combined total of 72)
Reserve the remainder of the prints.

From the remainder of the green prints, cut a *combined total* of:
16 rectangles, 2½" x 6½"

From red print #1, cut:
1 strip, 6½" x 42"; crosscut into 4 squares, 6½" x 6½". From the remainder of the strip, cut 9 squares, 2½" x 2½".

From red print #2, cut:
72 rectangles, 1½" x 2½"

From the dark-red print, cut:
72 squares, 1½" x 1½"

From *each* of the 16 assorted prints, cut:
5 rectangles, 2½" x 6½" (combined total of 80)
1 square, 2½" x 2½" (combined total of 16)
8 squares, 1½" x 1½" (combined total of 128)
Keep the squares organized by print.

From the dark-brown print, cut:
7 binding strips, 2½" x 42"
4 strips, 1½" x 23½"
4 strips, 1½" x 24½"

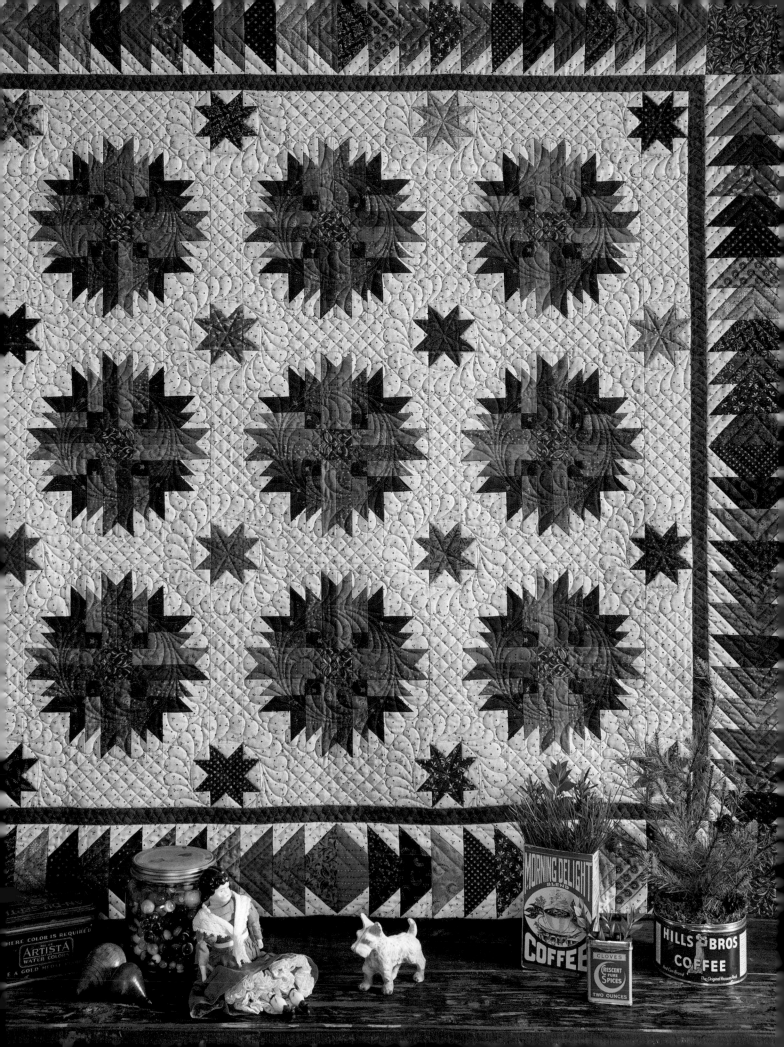

FINISHED QUILT SIZE: 60½" x 60½"

FINISHED BLOCK SIZE: 12" x 12"

Designed by Kim Diehl. Pieced by Jennifer Martinez and Kim Diehl.
Machine quilted by Deborah Poole.

Piecing the Wreath Blocks

Sew all pieces with right sides together using a ¼" seam allowance unless otherwise noted.

1. Use a pencil and an acrylic ruler to draw a diagonal sewing line from corner to corner on the wrong side of 72 tan 1½" squares.

2. Layer a prepared tan 1½" square onto one end of a green 1½" x 5½" rectangle. Stitch the pair together on the drawn line. Refer to "Pressing Triangle Units" on page 107 to fold, press, and trim the layers. Repeat for a total of 36 long green rectangles and 36 long green mirror-image rectangles measuring 1½" x 5½", including the seam allowances.

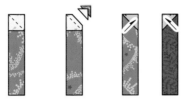

Make 36 of each.

3. Layer a tan 1½" x 2½" rectangle and a green 1½" x 3½" rectangle together as shown. Fold back the end of the tan strip that extends beyond the green strip, aligning the fold to be flush with the edge of the green strip it's resting upon; finger-press the crease. Unfold the tan strip. Align the edge of an acrylic ruler with the fold at the top of the tan strip, positioning the lower ruler edge at the opposite corner of the tan strip. Use a pencil to draw a straight line from the top of the tan strip to the opposite corner. Pin the marked layers together. Stitch the pair together on the drawn line. Trim away the excess layers at the corner of the diagonal seam, leaving a ¼" seam allowance. Fold the tan rectangle open to form a pieced rectangle. Repeat for a total of 36 pieced short green rectangles and 36 pieced short green

mirror-image rectangles measuring 1½" x 4½", including the seam allowances.

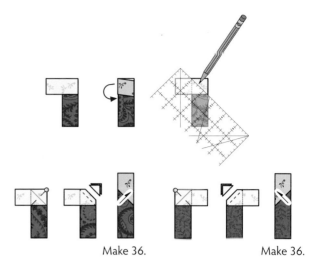

Make 36.   Make 36.

4. Using the red-print #2 and tan 1½" x 2½" rectangles, repeat step 3 to make 36 pieced red rectangles and 36 pieced red mirror-image rectangles measuring 1½" x 3½", including the seam allowances.

Make 36.   Make 36.

5. Lay out one tan 3½" square, one pieced red rectangle, one pieced red mirror-image rectangle, and one dark-red 1½" square in two horizontal rows as shown. Join the pieces in each row. Press the seam allowances away from the pieced rectangles. Join the rows. Press the seam allowances toward the row with the tan square. Repeat for a total of 36 pieced squares measuring 4½" square, including the seam allowances.

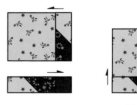

Make 36.

6. Join a pieced short green rectangle to a step 5 pieced square as shown. Press the seam allowances away from the newly added rectangle. Join a dark-red 1½" square to the green end of a pieced short green mirror-image rectangle. Press the seam allowances toward the red square. Join this unit to the edge of the step 5 square, adjacent to the previously added rectangle. Press the seam allowances away from the newly added rectangle. Repeat for a total of 36 corner units measuring 5½" square, including the seam allowances.

Make 36.

7. Join a pieced long green rectangle and a pieced long green mirror-image rectangle as shown. Press the seam allowances to one side, choosing the side that will result in the best inner point. Repeat for a total of 36 green units measuring 2½" x 5½", including the seam allowances.

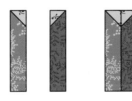

Make 36.

8. Lay out four corner units, four green units, and one 2½" red-print #1 square in three horizontal rows as shown. Join the pieces in each row. Press the seam allowances of the top and bottom rows away from the green units. Press the seam allowances of the middle row toward the red print. Join the rows. Press the seam allowances away from the middle row. Repeat for a total of nine Wreath blocks measuring 12½" square, including the seam allowances.

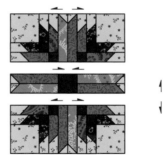 

Make 9.

Piecing the Star-Point Units

1. Use a pencil and an acrylic ruler to draw a diagonal sewing line from corner to corner on the wrong side of each assorted 1½" square.

2. Select eight matching prepared 1½" squares. Layer a prepared square onto one end of a tan 1½" x 2½" rectangle as shown. Stitch the pair together on the drawn line. Refer to "Pressing Triangle Units" to fold, press, and trim the layers to form a star point. In the same manner, add a second prepared 1½" square to the remaining end of the tan rectangle to make a mirror-image point. Repeat for a total of four flying-geese star-point units from each print

to make a combined total of 64 units measuring 1½" x 2½", including the seam allowances.

Make 4 from each print
(combined total of 64).

Laying out the Quilt Center

1. Referring to the quilt pictured on page 98 and using a design wall or floor area, lay out the Wreath blocks in three horizontal rows of three blocks each, leaving a few inches of space between each one.

2. Lay out an assorted 2½" square at each corner of the blocks, positioning the colors in a way that pleases you. When you're happy with the arrangement, lay out a matching star-point unit on each side of the print squares.

3. Use the tan 3½" x 10½" rectangles to fill the open spaces between the star points around the entire perimeter of the quilt center.

4. Using the pictured quilt as a guide, position a tan 1½" square at each end of the star-point units that run along the outer edges of the quilt center.

5. Place a tan print 2½" x 10½" rectangle in each remaining open space between the blocks in the quilt center.

Piecing the Quilt Center

1. To assemble the top sashing row, join the tan 1½" squares, the star-point units, and the matching-print 2½" squares to make four partial star units. Press the seam allowances as shown. Place these partial star units back in their original positions.

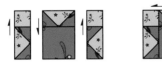

Make 4.

2. Join the partial star units from step 1 with the tan 3½" x 10½" rectangles to complete the top horizontal sashing row. Press the seam allowances toward the tan rectangles.

3. Repeat steps 1 and 2 to make the mirror-image bottom sashing row.

4. To make the far-left and far-right sashing units for each block row, join the tan 1½" squares to the star-point units they are resting next to. Press the seam allowances toward the tan squares. Join the point sides of these units to each end of the tan 3½" x 10½" rectangles they were positioned next to. Press the seam allowances toward the tan rectangles.

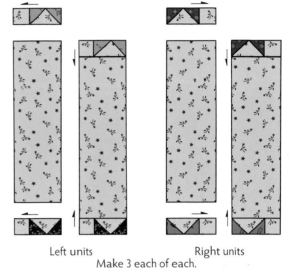

Left units   Right units
Make 3 each of each.

5. Join the point sides of the remaining star-point units in each block row to the tan 2½" x 10½" rectangles they are resting next to. Press the seam allowances toward the tan rectangles.

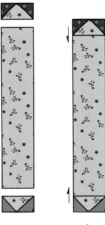

Make 6.

6. Join the pieces in each horizontal block row. Press the seam allowances away from the blocks.

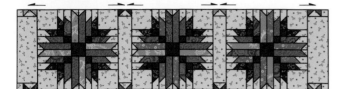

7. Stitch the pieces together in each of the two remaining horizontal sashing rows. Press the seam allowances away from the star points.

8. Using the pictured quilt as a guide, join the pieced horizontal rows to form the quilt center. Press the seam allowances toward the sashing rows. The pieced quilt center should now measure 46½" square, including the seam allowances.

Adding the Inner Border

1. Join two dark-brown 1½" x 23½" strips end to end. Press the seam allowances open. Repeat for a total of two pieced strips. Join these strips to the right and left sides of the quilt center.

2. Repeat step 1 using the dark-brown 1½" x 24½" strips and joining them to the top and bottom edges of the quilt center. The quilt top should now measure 48½" square, including the seam allowances.

Piecing and Adding the Outer Border

1. Using a pencil and an acrylic ruler, draw a diagonal sewing line from corner to corner on the wrong side of each tan 2½" square.

2. Using the assorted print and assorted green 2½" x 6½" rectangles and the prepared tan 2½" squares, follow step 2 of "Piecing the Star-Point Units" on page 100 to make a total of 96 flying-geese units with blunt tips measuring 2½" x 6½", including the seam allowances.

Make 96.

3. Lay out 12 flying-geese units in a left-facing position and 12 units in a right-facing position. Join the units. Press the seam allowances toward the wide ends of the flying-geese units. Press the center seam of the middle diamond open. Repeat for a total of four pieced border strips measuring 6½" x 48½", including the seam allowances.

Make 4.

4. Join a pieced border strip to the right and left sides of the quilt top. Press the seam allowances toward the inner border.

5. Join a 6½" red print #1 square to each end of the remaining pieced border strips. Press the seam allowances toward the red print. Join these strips to the remaining sides of the quilt top. Press the seam allowances toward the inner border. The pieced quilt top should now measure 60½" square, including the seam allowances.

Completing the Quilt

Layer the quilt top, batting, and backing. Quilt the layers. The featured quilt was machine quilted with feathered wreaths over each block and a diagonal crosshatch to fill the centers of the wreaths. The stars were stitched with diagonal lines from point to point to form an intersecting asterisk design. The open background areas of the quilt center were filled in with a diagonal crosshatch pattern, and the brown inner border was stitched with a ribbon candy design. The outer-border flying-geese units were stitched with repeating straight lines to form V patterns, with the lines extending onto the tan background areas of the border. Feathered wreaths were stitched onto the border corner squares, and the open wreath centers were filled with a diagonal crosshatch. Join the seven dark-brown 2½" x 42" strips into one length and use it to bind the quilt.

YULETIDE STYLE

Snow in a Jar

In keeping with my love of repurposing everyday items and using natural ingredients for my decorating, here's a fun and incredibly simple way to bring "snow" indoors. Use any large jar (from vintage apothecary jars to kitchen canning jars, anything will work!), and pour Epsom salt into the base before adding little Christmasy things— sprigs of greenery, pinecones, ornaments, even fresh cranberries. Sprinkle with more salt for a wintry look, and voila! Snow in a jar!

Kim's Quiltmaking Basics

This section provides tons of how-to information for the techniques and steps used to make the quilts and projects found in this book. For even more details, please visit ShopMartingale.com/HowtoQuilt, where you can download free illustrated guidelines.

Yardage Requirements

Project directions in this book assume the following usable dimensions for yardage and precut pieces after prewashing and removing selvages: yardage, 42" width; fat quarters, 18" x 21"; fat eighths, 9" x 21"; chubby sixteenths, 9" x 10½"; and charm squares, 5" x 5". To make the best use of your fabric, please cut your pieces in the order given.

Rotary Cutting

Unless otherwise noted, please cut all pieces on the straight of grain and across the width of the fabric. To speed the process of cutting my fabrics, I routinely fold my pressed fabric in half with the selvages together, and then in half once more.

To begin cutting, lay your fabric on a cutting mat with the folded cloth edge aligned with a horizontal line of the marked grid. Position the ruler onto the fabric, aligning the measurement lines with the mat grid, and make a vertical cut along one side of the cloth to establish a straight edge. Measure and cut your pieces, working out from this edge.

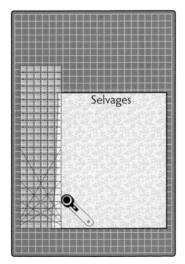

To cut half-square triangles from a square or layered stack of squares, lay your ruler diagonally across the square with the cutting edge directly over the corners, and make the cut.

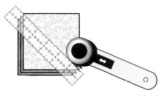

Cutting Bias Strips

Some projects in this book call for bias strips (lengths of cloth that have been cut diagonally rather than across the width of the fabric), which are usually used in projects that feature appliquéd stems and vines. The following steps are my preferred method for cutting these strips, as they result in a manageable size of cloth that produces strips approximately twice the cut length once they're unfolded. Another benefit of this method is that you can join the cut strips end to end to make one long length, and then cut the exact pieces you need from this joined strip, resulting in little or no waste.

1. After pressing the fabric smooth, lay it in a single layer on a large cutting mat. Grasp one corner of the fabric and fold it back to form a layered triangle of any size you choose, aligning the top straight edge with the straight grain of the bottom layer of fabric.

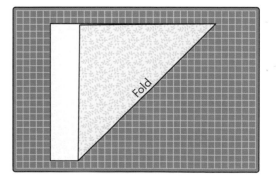

2. Rotate the layered pieced of cloth to align the folded edge with a cutting line on your mat, ensuring the fold is resting evenly along the marked line to prevent a dogleg curve in your strips after they've been cut and unfolded.

3. Use an acrylic ruler and rotary cutter to cut through the folded edge of cloth a few inches in from one pointed end. With the ruler aligned with the lines of your cutting mat, begin cutting your strips at measured intervals from this edge (as called for in your pattern instructions). If you reach the end of the folded edge of cloth and require additional strips, simply begin again at step 1 and repeat the process, using another corner of your cloth or squaring up the end from which you've been cutting.

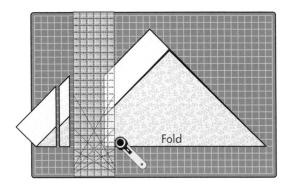

Fold

4. Square off the strip ends and trim them to the desired length, or sew multiple squared-off lengths together to achieve the length needed. Press the seam allowances to one side, all in the same direction. Experience has taught me that for strips which will be used for bias tube stems, joining the lengths with straight seams (rather than diagonal seams that are traditionally used) will enable you to easily press the stems flat with a bias bar, as it will slide through the sewn tubes easily without becoming caught on the diagonal seams.

Trim ends.

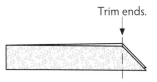

Pinning

I recommend pinning your patchwork at regular intervals, including all sewn seams and intersections, to keep the layers from shifting as they're joined. Be sure to place a pin at the back edge of each patchwork unit (where fishtailing can occur), as this will enable you

to lay your finger over the pin head to guide the unit under the presser foot in a straight line.

Machine Piecing

Unless otherwise instructed, always join your fabrics with right sides together using a ¼" seam allowance. An accurate seam allowance is easy to achieve using a ¼" presser foot, or you can make a sewing guide using masking tape. Simply lower your sewing machine's needle until the point gently rests upon the ¼" line of an acrylic ruler, ensuring that it's resting in a straight position. Apply a line of ¼" masking tape to the sewing-machine surface exactly along the ruler's edge, taking care not to cover the feed dogs. Align the edge of the fabrics with this taped line as you feed the pieces through the machine.

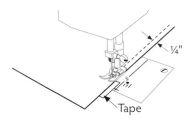

¼"

Tape

To achieve a sturdy, secure seam and more stitches per inch, I routinely shorten my stitch length (from 2.2 to 1.8 on my sewing machine).

Chain Piecing

For projects with many pieces to be joined, chain piecing is the perfect approach to increase your speed and conserve thread. Simply feed your patchwork through the sewing machine continuously without snipping the threads; after stitching, cut the threads between the units to separate them.

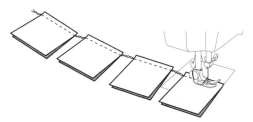

Pressing Seams

The importance of pressing is often minimized, but is a crucial step for achieving accurate patchwork with seams that lie smooth and flat. I recommend using a hot, dry iron to press as follows.

1. Place the patchwork on a firm-surfaced iron board with the fabric right sides together. Place the fabric you wish to press toward (usually the darker print) on top. On the wrong side of the fabric, briefly bring your iron down onto the sewn seam to warm the fabric.

2. Lift the iron and fold the top piece of fabric back to expose the right sides of the cloth. While the fabric is still warm, run your fingernail along the sewn thread line to relax the fibers at the fold and open the cloth all the way to the line of stitching; press the seam flat from the right side of the patchwork. The seam allowances will now lie under the fabric that was originally positioned on top.

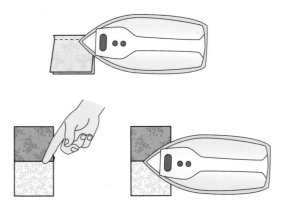

I recommend pressing patchwork without steam in case any adjustments are needed. Once my quilt top is complete, I give it a quick steam press or I apply a light misting of Mary Ellen's Best Press (this gives the cloth a fresh, crisp scent) before using my iron to set the seams firmly in place.

Pressing Triangle Units

For projects that call for stitch-and-fold triangles (made by folding open one corner of a diagonally stitched top square), I recommend the following steps.

1. Fold the top triangle back and align the corner with the corner of the bottom square or rectangle to keep it square; press in place.

2. Trim away the excess layers of fabric beneath the top triangle, leaving a ¼" seam allowance.

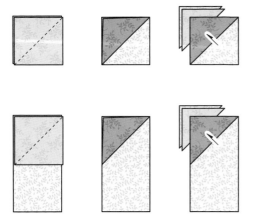

Traditionally, the excess fabric beneath the top triangle is trimmed *before* the unit is pressed, but I've found that this method of pressing and trimming produces more accurate patchwork that seldom requires squaring up.

Invisible Machine Appliqué

The results that can be achieved with invisible machine appliqué are fantastic because they closely resemble the look of needle-turn appliqué, but the process is much quicker. In addition to your standard quiltmaking supplies, you'll need the following tools and products for this method.

- .004 monofilament thread in smoke and clear colors
- Awl or stiletto tool with a *sharp* point
- Bias bars in various widths
- Embroidery scissors with a fine, sharp point
- Freezer paper
- Iron with a pointed pressing tip (travel-sized or mini appliqué irons work well for this technique)
- Liquid fabric glue, water soluble and acid free (my favorite brand is Quilter's Choice Basting Glue by Beacon Adhesives)
- Open-toe presser foot
- Pressing board with a *firm* surface
- Sewing machine with adjustable tension control, capable of producing a tiny zigzag stitch
- Size 75/11 (or smaller) machine-quilting needles
- Tweezers with rounded tips

Choosing Your Monofilament Thread

There are currently two types of monofilament thread (sometimes called invisible thread) that work well for invisible machine appliqué: nylon and polyester. Both types have their own characteristics and strengths and can bring different benefits to your appliqué projects.

In my experience, nylon thread tends to produce results that are slightly more invisible, but extra care should be used while your project is being assembled and pressed because nylon can be weakened by the heat of a very hot iron. For best results when working with nylon thread, avoid applying prolonged or high heat directly to the front of your appliqués and press any nearby seams with care. Once the project is finished and bound, I've found that the stitched appliqués will stand up well to everyday use and care. When I use nylon monofilament for my own projects, I've had very good results using the YLI brand.

If you'd like to feel confident that your appliqués will remain securely in place, even if they're inadvertently pressed from the front and exposed to direct heat from your iron, you may wish to use polyester monofilament thread. I find that the look of polyester monofilament can vary greatly from one brand to another, with some appearing less transparent or even shinier than others. Depending upon the brand you choose, the monofilament may be slightly more visible on your stitched appliqués. For projects where I've opted to use a polyester product I've been very pleased with the Sulky brand, because I feel the results most closely resemble those that are achieved when using nylon.

Ultimately, it's best to experiment with both types of monofilament and make this decision based upon your own personal results.

Preparing Pattern Templates

For projects featuring multiple appliqués made from one pattern, I've found that being able to trace around a sturdy template to make the pieces needed, rather than tracing over the pattern sheet numerous times, speeds the process tremendously. Keep in mind that complex shapes can be modified to fit your skill level—simply fatten up thin tips or redraw narrow inner curves to make them more friendly. Your end result will look essentially the same, but your shapes will be much easier to work with.

Any time a template is used, only one will be needed, because it's simply a tracing tool to easily duplicate the pattern shape for the remaining appliqué steps. I recommend making templates from freezer paper (which eliminates the need to buy template plastic) using these steps.

1. Cut a single piece of freezer paper about twice as large as your shape. Use a pencil to trace the pattern onto one end of the nonwaxy side of the paper. Fold the freezer paper in half, waxy sides together, and use a hot, dry iron (I place mine on the cotton setting) to fuse the folded paper layers together.

2. Cut out the shape on the drawn line, taking care to duplicate it accurately.

Preparing Paper Pattern Pieces

Pattern pieces are used differently than pattern templates, as these individual paper shapes will be used to prepare the appliqués from cloth. Always cut paper pattern pieces on the drawn lines, as the seam allowances will be added later when the shapes are cut from fabric. As you cut your paper pattern pieces, I suggest moving the paper, rather than the scissors, to achieve smooth, flowing edges.

Use the prepared template (or pattern sheet, if you're preparing fewer than a dozen pieces) to trace the number of pattern pieces needed onto the nonwaxy side of a piece of freezer paper. To easily make multiple pattern pieces, stack the freezer paper (up to eight layers deep for simple shapes, and four to six layers deep for more complex shapes) with the waxy sides facing down; anchor the shape centers using pins to prevent shifting or use staples at regular intervals slightly outside the shape in the background. Cut out the pattern pieces on the drawn lines and discard the background areas.

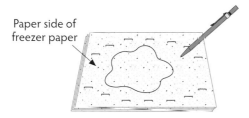

Paper side of freezer paper

Mirror-image shapes are easy to prepare; trace the pattern onto the nonwaxy side of one end of a strip of freezer paper, and then fold it accordion style in widths to fit your shape. Anchor the layers together as previously described and cut out the shape. When you separate the pieces every other shape will be a mirror image.

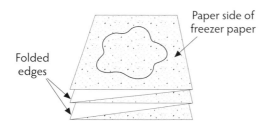

Paper side of freezer paper

Folded edges

I consistently use this accordion-fold technique for any shapes without an obvious direction, even if they're not perfectly symmetrical, because it speeds my progress and makes the quilt design more interesting. Multiple pattern pieces for shapes that do have an obvious direction (such as a bird) should be prepared by stacking individual freezer-paper pieces waxy side down as described previously.

PIN POINT

Shape Shortcut

If you're preparing your appliqué pattern pieces using purchased freezer-paper sheets created specifically for quiltmaking, here's a great little shortcut for easily transferring the shapes for cutting. Rather than tracing the patterns, use your inkjet printer to photocopy the pattern page onto the dull paper side of a single sheet of freezer paper. (For my copier, I load the freezer paper into the tray with the waxy side down; you may wish to do a quick test to determine the direction of the paper needed for your own copier by marking a sheet of paper with an x and taking note of your results after the sheet runs through the printer.) Cut the individual shapes from the copied sheet of freezer paper a little bit outside the lines, pin or staple them to the top of the accordion-folded freezer-paper strip or stack, and then proceed as previously instructed to cut out the shape on the copied lines. This little trick is a super timesaver because it eliminates the need for tracing and makes it easy to achieve accurately duplicated shapes.

Preparing Appliqués

1. Apply a small amount of fabric glue stick to the center of the dull paper side of each pattern piece before affixing it to the wrong side of the fabric, shiny side *up*, leaving approximately ½" between each shape for seam allowances. I generally position the longest lines or curves of each shape on the diagonal because the resulting bias edges are easier to work with than straight-grain edges when pressing the seam allowances over onto the paper pattern pieces.

Waxy side of freezer paper up

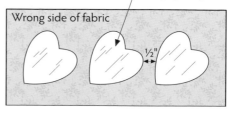

Wrong side of fabric

2. Using embroidery scissors, cut out each shape, adding an approximate ¼" seam allowance around the paper. For this technique, I've learned that more is actually better when it comes to seam allowances, as cutting too scant a seam allowance will make the fabric more difficult to work with. Any seam-allowance section that feels too bulky can be trimmed a bit, but you can't make scant seam allowances bigger.

When turning seam allowances to the back of an appliqué to press and finish the edges, I've discovered that it's actually better to leave the seam allowances of outer curves and points unclipped. The seam allowances of inner points or pronounced inner curves should be clipped once at the center position, stopping two or three threads away from the paper edge. If you're unsure whether an inner curve is pronounced enough to need a clip, try pressing it without one—if the fabric easily follows the shape of the curve and lies flat, you've eliminated a step!

Clip inner points
to paper edge.

Pressing Appliqués

The steps that follow will help you produce finished appliqués with smoothly turned-under edges that closely resemble needle turn. Keep in mind that for each shape, you'll want to work along the appliqué edge on the side that's farthest away from you, rotating the appliqué toward the point of your iron as you work in one direction from start to finish.

The smaller the shape or curvier the edges are, the smaller the increments should be as you rotate and press your way around the piece. This will enable the fabric to smoothly hug the shape of your appliqué for smooth, flawless results. Always begin pressing along a straight edge or a gentle curve, never at a point or a corner, and rotate the appliqué toward the iron as previously suggested, because this will direct the seam allowance of any points toward your "smart" hand (which you'll later use to hold the awl or stiletto to fine-tune and finish any points).

1. Beginning at a straight or gently curved edge and working your way around the entire shape in one direction, use the pad of your finger to smooth the fabric seam allowances over onto the waxy side of the paper pattern piece, following with the point of a hot, dry iron (I place my iron on the cotton setting) and *firmly* press it in place. The weight of the iron will work together with the heat to anchor the seam to the pattern piece. To avoid puckered appliqué edges, always draw the seam allowances slightly backward toward the last section pressed. I routinely let the point of my iron rest on each newly pressed section of seam allowance, holding it in place as I draw the next section over onto the paper pattern piece. Allowing the iron to rest in place while you work will lengthen the amount of time the fabric receives heat, and it will help the cloth to fuse more firmly to the paper.

2. For sharp outer points, press the seam allowances so the folded edge of the fabric extends beyond the first side of the pattern point, snugging the fabric firmly up against the paper edge. Fold over the seam allowance of the remaining side of the point and continue pressing. After the seam allowance of the entire piece has been pressed, apply a small amount of glue stick to the bottom of the folded flap of fabric seam allowance at the point. If the seam-allowance flap will be visible from the front of the appliqué, use the point of an awl or stiletto to drag the fabric in and away from the appliqué edge (not down from the point, as this will blunt it) and touch it with the point of a hot iron to heat set the glue and fuse it in place. For narrow points, I like to roll the seam allowances under slightly as I draw them in from the edge with the awl; this will enable the seams to be completely hidden from the front of the appliqué.

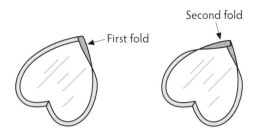

Second fold

First fold

One more tip I'd like to share to help achieve the beautiful sharp appliqué points we all strive for, is to ensure that your pressed seam allowance hugs the paper edge on both sides of any given point. I've often found that when a point is less than perfect, it's because the fabric seam allowance has flared away from the paper pattern piece, resulting in a mushy point. Ensuring the cloth always hugs the pattern piece will help produce crisp, precise points.

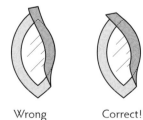

Wrong   Correct!

3. To prepare an inner point or pronounced inner curve, stop pressing the seam allowances just shy of the center clipped section. Reaching under the appliqué at the clip, use the pad of your finger or the point of an awl to draw the clipped section of fabric snugly onto the paper, following immediately with the iron to fuse the cloth onto the paper.

Always turn your prepared appliqué over to the front to evaluate your pressing and adjust any areas that could be improved. Tiny imperfections can be smoothed by nudging them with the point of your hot iron, and more pronounced imperfections can be loosened and re-pressed from the back.

Making Bias-Tube Stems and Vines

To achieve finished stems and vines that can be curved flawlessly and don't require the seam allowances to be turned under, I use bias tubes. After cutting the strips specified in the project instructions (and referring to "Cutting Bias Strips" on page 105 for guidelines), prepare them as follows.

1. With *wrong* sides together, fold the strip in half lengthwise and stitch a scant ¼" from the long raw edges to form a tube. (I stitch my seams about two or three threads less than a true ¼", as this often eliminates the need to trim the seam allowances and allows the bias bar to slide through the sewn fabric tube more easily). For any stem sewn from a strip with a cut width of 1" or less, you'll likely need to trim the seam allowances to approximately ⅛" so they'll be hidden when the stem is viewed from the front.

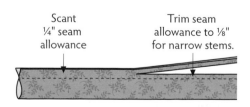

Scant ¼" seam allowance

Trim seam allowance to ⅛" for narrow stems.

2. Because seam-allowance differences can occur, the best bias-bar width for each project can vary from person to person, even for stems of the same size. Ultimately, I've found it's best to simply choose a bar that will fit comfortably into the sewn tube, and then slide it along as you press the stem flat to one side (not open), centering the seam allowances so they won't be visible from the front.

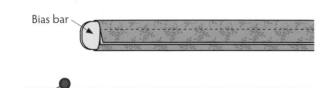

Bias bar

PIN POINT

Bias-Bar Bulk

Because of the thickness of bias bars, especially those made from plastic, it may sometimes appear that your seam allowance will be visible from the front of the stem after you've pressed the tube flat. Before taking on the added step of trimming the seam allowance, I've learned to routinely press the tube from the back a second time after removing the bias bar. This second press will remove the bulk of the bar and enable you to see at a glance the true resting position of the seam allowance.

3. Remove the bias bar and place small dots of liquid basting glue at approximately ½" to 1" intervals along the seam line underneath the layers of the pressed seam allowances; then use a hot, dry iron on the wrong side of the stem, allowing it to rest on each area of the stem for two or three seconds to heat set the glue and fuse the seam allowances in place.

Basting Appliqués

Invisible machine appliqué, like traditional hand appliqué, is sewn in layers from the bottom to the top. Keep in mind as you lay out and baste your appliqués that it's a good practice to leave approximately ½" between the outermost appliqués of your design and the raw edge of your background, because this will

preserve an intact margin of space around each piece after the quilt top has been assembled.

1. Lay out the prepared appliqués on the background to ensure that everything fits and is to your liking. As you lay out your pieces, remember that any appliqué with a raw edge that will be overlapped by another piece (such as a stem) should be overlapped by approximately ¼" to prevent fraying.

2. Remove all but the bottommost appliqués, and then baste them in place. Liquid basting glue for fabric is my preferred basting method because there are no pins to stitch around or remove and the appliqués will not shift or cause the background cloth to shrink as they're stitched. I suggest glue basting your appliqués as follows.

Without shifting the appliqué from its position, fold over one half of the shape to expose the back and place small dots of liquid basting glue along the fabric seam allowances (not the freezer-paper pattern piece) at approximately ½" to 1" intervals. Firmly push the glue-basted portion of the appliqué in place with your hand and repeat with the remaining half of the shape. From the back, use a hot, dry iron to heat set the glue.

Preparing Your Sewing Machine

Monofilament thread produces results that are nearly invisible and it's easy to use once you know how to prepare your sewing machine. Be sure to match your monofilament thread to your appliqué, not your background, choosing the smoke color for medium and dark prints and clear for bright colors and pastels. If you're not sure which color is the best choice, lay a strand of each thread over your print to audition the results. Whenever possible, use the upright spool pin position on your sewing machine for the monofilament, as this will facilitate a smooth, even feed.

1. Use a size 75/11 (or smaller) machine-quilting needle in your sewing machine and thread it with monofilament. I've discovered that prints with a subtle texture, and often batiks, can make needle holes more visible, so if this occurs, I recommend substituting a smaller needle.

2. Wind the bobbin with all-purpose, neutral-colored thread. In my experience, a 50-weight (or heavier) thread works well for this technique in most sewing machines, as it will resist sliding through the cloth and pulling up through the surface of your appliqués. Also, keep in mind that prewound bobbins, while convenient, can sometimes make it difficult to achieve perfectly balanced tension for this technique.

   Note: If your machine's bobbin case features a "finger" with a special eye for use with embroidery techniques or a coiled wire "pigtail," threading your bobbin thread through these openings will often provide additional tension control to perfectly regulate your stitches.

3. Program your sewing machine to the zigzag stitch, adjust the width and length to achieve a tiny stitch as shown below (keeping in mind that your inner stitches should land two or three threads inside your appliqué, with your outer stitches piercing the background immediately next to the appliqué), and reduce the tension setting. For many sewing machines, a width, length, and tension setting of 1 produces the perfect stitch.

⌇⌇⌇⌇⌇⌇⌇⌇⌇⌇⌇⌇⌇⌇⌇

Approximate stitch size

Stitching the Appliqués

Before stitching your first invisible-machine-appliqué project, I recommend experimenting with a simple pattern shape to become comfortable with this technique and find the best settings for your sewing machine. Keep your test piece as a quick reference for future projects, making a note directly on the background fabric as to your machine's stitch width, stitch length, and tension settings. Also, if you routinely use more than one type of thread in your bobbin, you should make a note of the thread that was used for your test piece—if the thread in your bobbin is changed for a different type, the balance of your components may change as well, and your settings may need to be adjusted.

1. Slide the basted appliqué under the sewing machine needle from front to back to direct the threads behind the machine, positioning it to the left of the needle.

2. Beginning at a straight or gently curved edge, place your fingertip over the monofilament tail or grasp the threads as your machine takes two or

three stitches. Release the threads and continue zigzag stitching around your shape, with your inner stitches landing on the appliqué and your outer stitches piercing the background immediately next to the appliqué. Train your eyes to watch the outer stitches while you sew to keep your appliqué positioned correctly and the inner stitches will naturally fall into place. After a short distance, pause and carefully clip the monofilament tail close to the background.

Stitch your appliqué at a slow to moderate speed to maintain good control, stopping and pivoting as often as needed to keep the edge of your shape feeding straight toward the needle. Whenever possible, pivot with the needle down inside the appliqué, because the paper pattern piece will stabilize the shape and prevent it from stretching or becoming distorted.

- If dots of bobbin thread appear along the top surface edge of your appliqué as you stitch, further adjust the tension settings on your machine (usually lower) until they disappear.

- Your machine's stitch should look like a true zigzag pattern on the wrong side of your work. If the monofilament thread is visible underneath your appliqué from the back, or the stitches appear loose or loopy, adjust the tension settings (usually higher) until they are secure.

PIN POINT

Continuous Thread Path

Years ago when I was developing my invisible machine-appliqué technique and learning the ins and outs of this timesaving method, I would stitch my stems and vines for any given design first, and then add the leaves. This approach required that I jumped from leaf to leaf as each one was stitched, resulting in a lot of extra time and wasted thread. In my own defense, I didn't know any better! I've since realized that positioning the points of my leaves so they just barely meet the stem or vine gives me the ability to have a continuous thread path while I appliqué the design. When I begin, I simply stitch along the stem until I arrive at a leaf, and then stitch around the leaf until I arrive back at the point where it touches the stem, and then continue on. This approach eliminates the need for a lot of starts and stops, and it saves a tremendous amount of thread.

3. To firmly secure an inner appliqué point, stitch to the position where the inner stitch rests exactly on the inner point of the appliqué and stop. Pivot the fabric, and with the appliqué inner point at a right angle to the needle, continue stitching. For pieces with inner points that seem delicate, I often give a little resistance to my piece as it's feeding under the needle and stitch the area twice to secure it well.

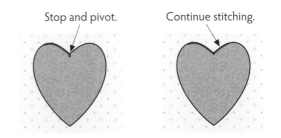

Stop and pivot.   Continue stitching.

4. To secure an outer point, stitch to the position where the outer stitch lands exactly next to the appliqué point in the background and stop. Pivot the fabric and continue stitching along the next side

of the shape. As you begin sewing again, a second stitch will drop into the point of the appliqué.

Stop and pivot.   Continue stitching.

5. Continue stitching around the edge of the appliqué until you overlap your starting point by approximately ¼". End with a locking stitch if your machine offers this feature, placing it where it will be least visible. For machines without a locking stitch, extend your overlapped area to about ½" and your appliqué will remain well secured.

   I've discovered that using a locking stitch to finish each appliqué doesn't make your stitching more secure, it simply communicates to your sewing machine that you've finished your current task, enabling you to easily position your next piece for stitching because the needle will consistently align and begin in the same position.

6. From time to time, I suggest evaluating the stitch placement along your appliqué edges to ensure you're achieving the best possible results. To do this, hold a completed appliqué piece up to the light and view it with the light shining from behind. A properly stitched appliqué will have a ring of tiny needle holes encircling the appliqué in the background cloth. If your results appear different, then adjustments to the placement of your work under the needle should be made as you stitch future pieces.

String Appliqué

When two or more appliqués are in close proximity on the same layer, I recommend stitching your first appliqué as instructed in "Stitching the Appliqués" on page 113, but instead of clipping the threads when you finish, lift the presser foot and slide the background to the next appliqué without lifting it from the sewing-machine surface. Lower the presser foot and resume stitching the next appliqué, remembering to end with a locking stitch or overlap your starting position by ¼" to ½". After the cluster of appliqués has been stitched, carefully clip the threads between each.

Removing Paper Pattern Pieces

On the wrong side of the stitched appliqué, use embroidery scissors to carefully pinch and cut through the fabric approximately ¼" inside the appliqué seam. Trim away the background fabric, leaving a generous ¼" seam allowance. Grasp the appliqué edge between the thumb and forefinger of one hand and grab the seam allowances immediately opposite with the other hand. Give a gentle but firm tug to free the paper edge. Next, use your fingertip to loosen the glue anchoring the pattern piece to the fabric; peel away and discard the paper. Any paper that remains in the appliqué corners can be pulled out with a pair of tweezers. Please rest easy knowing that cutting away the fabric behind an appliqué won't weaken the quilt top in any way—this method of appliqué is very secure, and it produces finished quilts that are soft and pliable, even with multiple layers of cloth.

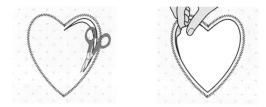

Completing the Machine-Appliqué Process

Working from the bottom layer to the top, continue basting and stitching the appliqués until each one has been secured in place, remembering to remove the paper pattern pieces before adding each new layer. Keep in mind that it isn't necessary to stitch any edge that will be overlapped by another piece. If needed, *briefly* press your finished work from the back to ensure the seam allowances lie smooth and flat. Always take care not to apply direct heat to the front of your appliqués, as this could weaken the monofilament threads.

Wool Appliqué

Wool is a really fun, fast, and forgiving fabric to work with, and I especially love the magic that happens when it's used in combination with traditional cotton fabrics. Wool that's been felted has a soft, densely woven feel to the cloth and it resists raveling as you work with it. I suggest that you use only 100% wool and, as a general rule, avoid worsted wool because it doesn't felt well and can be challenging to work with. You can usually identify worsted wool by its hard, flat weave, and you'll often find it used for garments such as men's suits.

For my method of appliquéing with wool, you'll need the following items in addition to your standard quiltmaking supplies:

- #8 or #12 perle cotton in colors to match or complement your wool
- Embroidery needle (a size 5 works well for me)
- Freezer paper
- Liquid basting glue, water soluble and acid free (my favorite brand is Quilter's Choice Basting Glue by Beacon Adhesives)
- Paper-backed fusible web (I like the results achieved when using HeatnBond Lite)
- Sharp scissors with a fine point
- Thimble

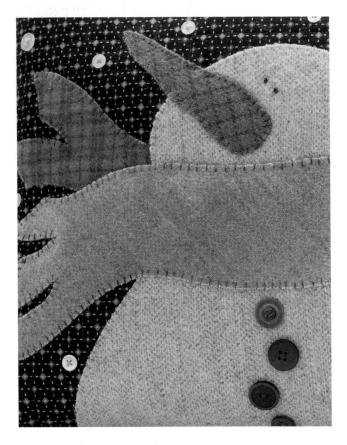

Felting Your Wool

If your wool hasn't been felted, this is easy to do. Wash similar-hued wool pieces in the washing machine on the longest cycle using a hot-water wash and a cold-water rinse. (You may wish to skim the surface of the water once or twice during the cycle to prevent loose fibers from clogging the drain.) Next, dry the wool in your dryer, again using the longest and hottest setting. Remove the dry wool promptly to help prevent wrinkles from forming.

As an added safety measure, I always wash and dry vividly colored pieces separately when I suspect they might lose dye, and I never wash wool that has been overdyed, because it will almost certainly bleed color—if I'm not sure whether a piece has been overdyed, I follow the rule that it's better to be safe and ask rather than to guess and be sorry. Finally, never wash wool that's been included as part of a kitted project, because it can continue to shrink and you may find yourself without enough wool to complete your project.

Preparing Wool Appliqués

When working with wool, I like to use a fusible-appliqué technique for the preparation steps, liquid fabric glue for basting the layers of wool together, and perle cotton and an embroidery needle to stitch the pieces. The combination of fusible web and the liquid glue produces ideal results because the fusible adhesive finishes and stabilizes the underside of the wool edges to reduce fraying, while the glue-basted edges hold the layers of wool together beautifully for easy stitching without pinning.

Keep in mind when you're using the following technique that your finished wool shapes will appear backward from the pattern and be reversed on your quilt if they are directional and aren't perfectly symmetrical.

1. Trace each appliqué shape the number of times indicated in the pattern instructions onto the paper side of your iron-on adhesive, leaving approximately ½" between each shape. For projects with numerous identical shapes (or nonsymmetrical shapes that need to be reversed), make a template as instructed in "Preparing Pattern Templates" on page 108 and use it to trace the required number of pieces. Remember that for this method you'll need one traced iron-on adhesive shape for each appliqué.

2. Cut out each shape approximately ¼" *outside* the drawn lines, and then cut away the center portion of the shape approximately ¼" *inside* the drawn lines to eliminate bulk and keep the shape pliable after the appliqué has been stitched. For added stability in large shapes, leave a narrow strip of

paper across the middle of the shape as you cut away the excess center portion; this will act as a bridge to connect the sides and prevent distortion as you lay out your shape on the wool.

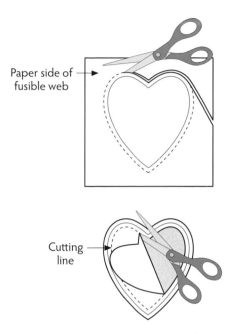

Paper side of fusible web

Cutting line

3. Following the manufacturer's instructions, fuse each shape, paper side *up*, to the *wrong* side of the fabric. After the fabric has cooled, cut out each shape exactly on the drawn lines. To protect the fusible adhesive and prevent the fabric appliqué edges from fraying, I suggest leaving the paper backing on your prepared pieces until you're ready to use them. To easily remove the paper backing, loosen an inside edge of the paper with a needle and peel it away.

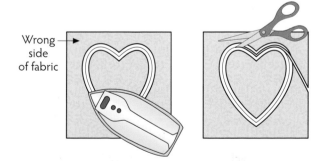

Wrong side of fabric

Stitching Wool Appliqués

After much experimenting, I've decided that the overhand stitch is my preferred method of appliquéing wool shapes because it's quick to stitch, uses less thread, and the stitches stay in place without rolling over the appliqué edge.

Whenever possible, I work from the top layer to the bottom to stitch any layered wool pieces into units (such as a stack of pennies) *before* adding them to my background, because this simplifies the sewing process and eliminates the need to stitch through multiple heavy layers of wool. Once the layered units have been sewn together, the appliqué designs can be stitched to the background, working from the bottom layer to the top.

1. Lay out your appliqués, including any stitched appliqué units, onto your background to ensure everything fits and is to your liking. Remove all but the bottom pieces. Remove the paper backing on each remaining piece and glue baste them in place, referring to "Basting Appliqués" on page 112 and applying small dots of liquid glue directly to the narrow margin of fusible adhesive that rims each shape.

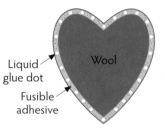

Liquid glue dot

Wool

Fusible adhesive

2. Use an embroidery needle threaded with a single knotted strand of #8 or #12 perle cotton to overhand stitch the pieces in place as shown below.

Overhand stitch

3. Remove the paper backings from the appliqués needed for the next layer of the design. Position, baste, and stitch the shapes in place, ensuring that any appliqué overlapping another piece does so by at least ¼". Continue working from the bottom layer to the top in this manner to complete the appliqué design, keeping in mind that it isn't necessary to cut away the backs of any appliqués stitched from wool.

Laundering Quilts that Include Wool

I'm frequently asked if quilts that include wool can be laundered, and the short answer is: of course! Using felted wool means that additional shrinkage of the wool cloth, if any, should be minimal. If my quilt contains wool pieces that have been overdyed, I take the precautionary step of using cold-water wash and rinse cycles, and also include a Color Catcher. Next, I dry the quilt using a low dryer setting or simply smooth it flat to slowly air dry. Easy!

Decorative Stitches

The decorative stitches used for the projects in this book are simple and easy, even for beginners! To make the stitches, use a size 5 embroidery needle and a single strand of #8 or #12 perle cotton, and follow these illustrations.

French knot

Stem stitch

Yo-Yos

Yo-yos are one of my favorite embellishments because they can be used for a variety of projects to add a subtle dimensional element. Best of all, they're a great way to use leftover scraps, and their small size makes them portable for some fun hand stitching on the go.

Select a yo-yo fabric circle. With the wrong side up, turn a ¼"-wide portion of the edge toward you to create a hem (just estimate this!). Using a knotted length of perle cotton and the embroidery needle, bring the needle up through the hem from the wrong side to hide the knot between the layers. Sew a running stitch as shown, with your stitches approximately ¼" long. Continue turning the hem to the front and stitching as you work your way around the circle to the starting point. Gently pull the thread to gather the yo-yo edges to the center. Insert the needle under the gathered edge, just to one side of the center opening, and bring it out on the back of the yo-yo. Knot and clip the thread, keeping the gathers pulled taut.

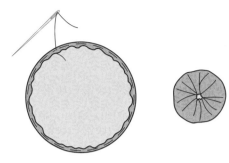

Completing the Quilt Top

Once the individual components of your quilt have been finished, assembling the blocks and adding your borders is the next step. The information that follows will help simplify and streamline this process.

Assembling the Quilt Center

Lay out your blocks or units, evaluating their placement and making any necessary changes; I suggest positioning blocks or units with strong hues into your corners to visually anchor and define the quilt center.

For greater ease when assembling large tops, I suggest joining the rows in groups of two or three. Next, join the grouped rows, working from the top and bottom edges toward the middle until you join all the rows.

Adding Borders

When joining border strips to the center of a quilt, fold each border piece in half to find the midpoint, and then finger-press a crease. Next fold each side of the quilt center in half and crease these midpoint positions as well. Align the creases of your individual components and pin them together for a perfect fit.

All of the measurements provided in this book for whole-cloth borders are mathematically correct, but because there is little or no stretch to these pieces when they've been cut from the lengthwise grain, you may wish to slightly increase the designated lengths. I routinely increase the length of my strips by ½" for borders measuring up to 60" long and by 1" for strips in excess of 60"; any excess length can be trimmed away after the borders are added.

Finishing Techniques

There are many choices available as you work through the final steps of your project—tailoring these decisions to suit your individual preferences will result in a finished quilt that reflects your own unique tastes and personality.

Batting

For quilt tops sewn from prewashed fabrics, I suggest using polyester batting or a cotton/polyester blend; this will ensure minimal shrinkage when your quilt is laundered. If your quilt top is stitched from fabrics that weren't prewashed, I'd recommend choosing cotton batting, particularly if you love the slightly puckered look of vintage quilts. For best results, always follow the manufacturer's instructions.

Backing

I cut and piece my quilt backings to be approximately 3" larger than my quilt top on all sides. As you consider choices for your backing, remember that prints with a lot of texture will make your quilting less visible, while muted prints and solids will emphasize your quilting design. To prevent shadowing, use fabrics in colors similar to those in your quilt top.

For the best use of your yardage, I suggest seaming your quilt backings as shown.

Lap quilts
up to 74" square

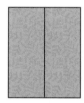

Twin-size bed quilts
up to 74" wide

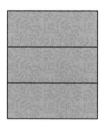

Full- and queen-size
bed quilts
up to 90" wide

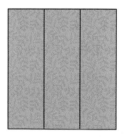

King-size bed quilts
up to 107" wide

Basting

To prepare your finished top for the quilting process, please use the steps that follow.

1. Place the backing fabric, wrong side up, on a large, flat surface. Smooth away any wrinkles and secure the edges with masking tape.

2. Center the batting on the backing fabric and smooth away any wrinkles.

3. Carefully center the quilt top on the layered batting and backing. For hand quilting, use white thread to baste diagonally from corner to corner, and then at 3" to 4" intervals as shown. For machine quilting, pin baste using size 2 rustproof safety pins and work from the center outward at 4" to 5" intervals as shown. Last, thread baste the edges.

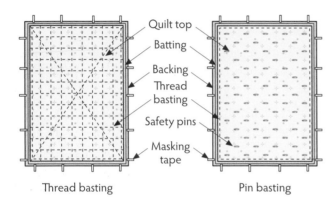

Quilt top
Batting
Backing
Thread basting
Safety pins
Masking tape

Thread basting   Pin basting

Marking Quilting Designs

Masking tape in various widths works beautifully as a guide for stitching straight quilting lines, but always remember to remove the tape at the end of each day to prevent adhesive from damaging your fabric. More elaborate designs can be marked on the top using a quilter's pencil or a fine-tipped water-soluble marker—doing this before the layers are assembled will provide a smooth marking surface and produce the best results. Blue markers work well for light- and medium-hued fabrics, while white markers work perfectly for medium- and dark-hued prints. For a beautiful finish, always ensure your quilt features an abundant and evenly spaced amount of quilting.

Hand Quilting

To hand quilt your project, place the layered quilt top in a hoop or frame and follow these steps.

1. Thread your needle with an approximately 18" length of quilting thread and knot one end. Insert the needle into the quilt top about 1" from where you wish to begin quilting, sliding it through the layers and bringing it up through the top; gently tug until the knot is drawn down into the layer of batting.

2. Take small, even stitches through the layers until you near the end of the thread. Make a knot in the thread about ⅛" from the quilt top. Insert and slide the needle through the batting layer, bringing it back up about 1" beyond your last stitch. Tug gently until the knot disappears and carefully clip the thread.

Hand-quilting stitch

Big-Stitch Quilting

Big-stitch quilting (sometimes called a utility stitch) is one of my favorite methods because it's a quick and easy way to include hand stitching on my projects without the huge time commitment that traditional hand quilting can require. For this style of quilting I use a size 5 embroidery needle and #8 or #12 perle cotton to sew a running stitch (with each stitch approximately ⅛" to a scant ¼" long) through the quilt layers, ending my stitches as I would for traditional hand quilting.

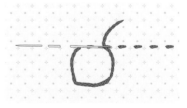

Perfectly Positioned Knots

It can be challenging to perfectly position the knot in your thread as you prepare to end your stitching, so here's a great little trick that consistently works for me. I make the loop that will form my knot near the quilt-top surface, and then place my needle in the loop as I slowly begin to pull it tight. As the loop begins to shrink, I slide my needle down the length of thread (while it's still in the loop) to steer the tightening knot right to the sweet spot. Works every time!

Machine Quilting

For in-depth machine-quilting instructions, please refer to *Machine Quilting with Style* (Martingale, 2015) by Christa Watson or *The Ultimate Guide to Machine Quilting* (Martingale, 2016) by Angela Walters and Christa Watson.

When an overall style of quilting is my best choice to add subtle texture without introducing another design element into my project mix, I use a swirling pattern.

To stitch this versatile design, sew a free-form circle of any size, and then fill in the center with ever-reducing concentric circles (think cinnamon rolls). When you arrive at the center, stitch a gentle wavy line to the next area to be swirled and continue filling the block or top, staggering the placement and size of the swirls, until the stitching is complete.

Start here.

Blended Quilting Styles

Never be afraid to blend small touches of hand quilting along with your machine quilting! Machine quilting enables your project to be quickly finished, while the hand-quilted accents, especially big-stitch accents, are quick to add and provide a huge return for a minimal investment of time. When I decide to take this blended approach, I let my machine quilter know which appliqués I plan to hand quilt so she can leave an approximate ¼" margin around them, or I'll sometimes indicate portions of blocks that I'd like to accent. After the bulk of the project has been machine quilted, it's a snap to add my own hand stitching because the top has been stabilized without any further action on my part. Best of all, your eye is truly drawn to the hand quilting and it's a wonderful way of keeping this traditional art form alive.

Binding

Traditionally, a 2½"-wide French-fold binding is used to finish most quilts. When I bind my quilts, however, I prefer a more unconventional method using 2"-wide strips that result in a traditional look from the front while producing a "chubby" border of color to frame the backing and add a pop of color. The binding yardage for each project will accommodate either method, with enough binding to encircle the quilt perimeter plus approximately 10" for mitered corners.

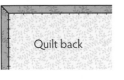
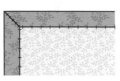

Traditional
French-fold binding   Chubby binding

Traditional French-Fold Binding

1. With right sides together, join the 2½"-wide strips end to end at right angles, stitching diagonally across the corners to make one long strip. Trim the seam allowances to ¼" and press them open.

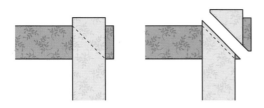

2. Cut one end at a 45° angle and press it under ¼". Fold the strip in half lengthwise, wrong sides together, and press.

3. After pinning the binding to the quilt top and beginning along one side of the quilt top (not a corner), use a ¼" seam allowance to stitch the binding along the raw edges. Stop sewing ¼" from

the first corner and backstitch. Clip the thread and remove the quilt from under the presser foot.

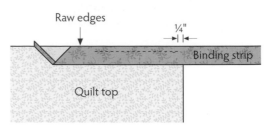

4. Make a fold in the binding, bringing it up and back down onto itself to square the corner. Rotate the quilt 90° and reposition it under the presser foot. Resume sewing at the top edge of the quilt, continuing around the perimeter in this manner.

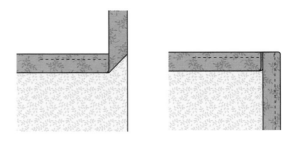

5. When you approach your starting point, cut the binding end at an angle 1" longer than needed and tuck it inside the previously sewn binding to enclose the raw end. Complete the stitching.

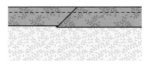

6. Bring the folded edge of the binding to the back of the quilt, enclosing the raw edges. Use a blind stitch and matching thread to hand sew the binding to the back. At each corner, fold the binding to form a miter and hand stitch it in place.

Chubby Binding

For this method, you'll need a bias-tape maker designed to produce 1"-wide, double-fold tape. For most of my quilts, I prefer to use binding strips that have been cut on the straight of grain, rather than the bias, because I feel this gives my quilt edges added stability. For scrappy bindings pieced from many prints of different lengths, I love the look achieved when the strips are joined end to end using straight seams.

1. Cut the strips 2" wide and join them end to end without pressing the seams. Next, slide the pieced strip through the bias-tape maker, pressing the folds with a hot, dry iron as they emerge so the raw edges meet in the center. As the tape maker slides along the pieced strip, the seams will automatically be directed to one side as they are pressed, resulting in one less step!

2. Open the fold of the strip along the top edge only. Turn the beginning raw end under ½" and finger-press the fold. Starting along one side of the quilt top (not a corner), align the unfolded raw edge of the binding with the raw edge of the quilt and pin in place as instructed in steps 3 and 4 of the French-fold method on page 122.

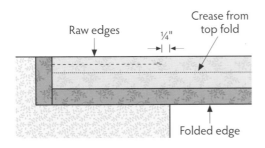

Raw edges ¼" Crease from top fold

Folded edge

3. When you approach your starting point, cut the end to extend 1" beyond the folded edge and complete the stitching.

4. Bring the wide folded edge of the binding to the back and hand stitch it (including the mitered folds at the corners) as instructed in step 6 of the French-fold method. The raw end of the strip will now be encased within the binding.

Attaching a Quilt Label

To document your work, remember to prepare a fabric quilt label including any information you'd like to share, and then hand stitch it to the back of your quilt.

About the Author

After falling in love with a sampler quilt pattern in the late 1990s, Kim impulsively purchased it, worked her way through the instructions to teach herself the needed steps, and realized she was smitten with quiltmaking.

Kim's second quilt was of her own design, and with her third quilt, she became the winner of *American Patchwork & Quilting* magazine's 1998 Pieces of the Past quilt challenge, turning her life down a new and unexpected path. With just her fourth quilt, Kim began publishing her original designs, and her work has been featured in numerous national and international quilting magazines.

Kim's favorite quilts include traditionally inspired patchwork designs, especially when combined with appliqué, and she loves stitching her quilts using modern techniques for an ideal blend of simplicity, ease, and charm. The popularity of her designs and quiltmaking methods led to an extensive teaching schedule for several years, until she retired from travel in 2015.

In addition to authoring her "Simple" series of books with Martingale, Kim continues to design her signature scrappy-style fabric collections for Henry Glass & Co., as well as quilts and projects for her Simple Whatnots Club.

Having the opportunity to spend her days at home once again has given Kim newfound time for all of the things she loves most—designing and stitching, gardening, cooking, antiquing, and most especially, her puppies and grandbabies.

Needle-Turn Appliqué

Can't get enough of Kim Diehl? Here's an excerpt from her latest release, *Simple Appliqué!*

Needle turn is a traditional hand-stitched appliqué method that has long been favored by quiltmakers. For this technique, shapes are traced and cut from fabric and the seam allowances are turned under as the appliqués are stitched in place. If you enjoy the comfort of handwork and love projects that are portable, this is an ideal method for stitching your appliqué designs.

Materials

In addition to standard quiltmaking supplies, the following tools and products are needed for this method:

- Embroidery scissors with a fine, sharp point
- Fine-weight thread in colors to match your appliqués
- Freezer paper
- Marking tools, such as a quilter's silver pencil or fine-tip water-soluble marker
- Size 9 or 10 straw needles (or a size that fits comfortably in your hand)

  Note: Straw needles feature a longer length that's easy to grasp, and they enable you to turn under and stitch your appliqués neatly while maintaining a good level of control as you work with the appliqué fabric.

- Thimble (leather thimbles work well for this technique because they offer a degree of flexibility).

Preparing the Appliqués for Stitching

1. To easily trace the appliqué shapes for cutting and stitching, prepare a tracing template of each pattern in your project as instructed in "Preparing Pattern Tracing Templates" (page 9 in *Simple Appliqué*).

"*Four Patch Potpourri,*" from Homestyle Quilts, coauthored with Laurie Baker

"*Summertime Scatter Garden*" from Simple Seasons

2. Using a quilter's silver pencil or a fine-tip water-soluble marker (white markers show up well on medium and dark prints; blue markers are easily visible on lighter prints), lay the templates on the right side of the fabrics and trace the shapes exactly around the paper edges the number of times indicated by the pattern **(fig. 1)**. If you're tracing more than one shape onto the same fabric, leave at least ½" between the shapes. Typically, I position my shapes with the longest lines or curves on the diagonal grain of the cloth, because the resulting bias edges are easier to work with. However, if I wish to take advantage of directional prints or stripes, then I disregard this guideline and position the shapes in a way that pleases me.

3. Using embroidery scissors with a fine, sharp point, cut out the traced shapes, adding a scant ¼" seam allowance on all sides **(fig. 2)**.

Incorporating Bias-Tube Stems and Vines

As a matter of personal preference, I use bias-tube stems and vines for all of my appliqué designs, no matter what appliqué method I'm using, because they eliminate the need to turn under seam-allowance edges as the lengths are stitched to the background. To prepare bias tubes, refer to "Making Bias-Tube Stems and Vines" (page 18 in *Simple Appliqué*).

Laying Out and Stitching Needle-Turn Appliqué Designs

1. Lay out the appliqué design to ensure everything fits and is to your liking, leaving approximately ½" between the outermost appliqués and the edge of the background fabric. When you're pleased with the arrangement, remove all but the bottommost pieces. Pin or thread baste the appliqués in place, placing the pins or basting stitches well away from the outer edges where the shapes will be stitched **(fig. 3)**.

Fig. 1 Trace the template shape onto the right side of the fabric.

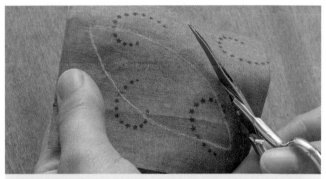
Fig. 2 Add a scant ¼" seam allowance as you cut out the traced shape.

Fig. 3 Pin or thread baste the appliqués to the background fabric.

Make sure your library of Kim Diehl books is complete!

Find these books and products at your friendly neighborhood quilt shop or at ShopMartingale.com.

Martingale®
Create with Confidence

Connect with us!